STRENGTH THROUGH KOI

THEY SAVED HITLER'S KOI AND OTHER STORIES

JONATHAN DOWNES

Edited by Jonathan Downes and Corinna James
Cover picture of Koi fish by Iggy Tavares
Cover and internal design by Mark North for CFZ Communications
Using Microsoft Word 2000, Microsoft , Publisher 2000, Adobe Photoshop CS.

First published in Great Britain by CFZ Press

CFZ Press
Myrtle Cottage
Woolfardisworthy
Bideford
North Devon
EX39 5QR

CFZ PRESS

ISBN: 978-1-905723-04-1

For Paul Whitrow,
because I always promised
that somehow
he would get into one
of my books

C**O**NTENT**S**

FOREWORD

When asked to write this introduction to the latest con-
tribution to great English literature penned by my old
friend Jonathan Downes, I was at a loss as to how to
describe the man.

I first came into contact with Jon some five years ago, when he
penned a column for a fishkeeping magazine to which I had
just been appointed Editor. I must say that he completely mis-
represented his importance to the said publication, but to my
shock and horror, I gradually gave him an increasingly large
amount of work.

Having known Jon telephonically for some months, I finally met
the creature itself at the infamous Weird Weekend.

We had agreed to transport scientist Chris Moiser to the event,
and I innocently asked: *"How shall I recognise Jon?"* Chris's answer was: *"Look for the Yeti with everything shaved but the
face."* Ah! So true!

The introductory lecture at my first Weird Weekend was led by
Dr Gail-Nina Anderson, who gave a talk on the `Influence of
the Vampire in Art`, whist wearing a black basque. I remember

thinking that all this would come apart at some stage, and I really wanted to be there when it happened. We later partook of an Ethiopian cream tea. (A cream tea served to us—and having been manufactured—by, a scion of the Imperial Ethiopian Royal family).

Having made the break, and decided to publish my own magazine, Jon offered himself the job of Deputy Editor and later informed me of this appointment. Since then, the two of us have oft worked late into the night on a diet of brandy and profanity.

As for Jon's koi credentials. You will read elsewhere in this book – should you get past this introduction – of his notorious - yet successful, attempt to achieve fame by claiming to be the man who saved Hitler's koi.

If nothing else it shows the gullibility of certain sections of the press.

May I also pay tribute to Jon's musical influences, which have ensured that a large percentage of the population of Devon are now tone deaf.

His rendition – along with his group which last consisted of various people who you might nervously edge away from if you met them in public – of *Elvis Died for our Sins* is interesting to say the least. The band goes downhill from there.

Jon presently resides in a small Devon village, which seems to have accepted him rather well, as 300 years ago he would undoubtedly have been burned as a suspected practitioner of the Satanic Arts. He has a fiancée, a collection of satellites, and his morning tea is brewed by a man who can officially claim to be a living god.

His hobbies include; strange life forms, punk music, and getting on my nerves.

It should also be mentioned that Jon has a fine nose for a good cocktail, but I intend to break that nose should he ever again offer me the concoction infamously known as a Salty Dog, which has a taste reminiscent of alcohol and polluted seawater.

STRENGTH THR⊕UGH K⊕I

In conclusion: May I unreservedly recommend this fine book to you, Dear Reader, even though I have not yet read it, and probably never will. No doubt you will be amused, educated, and other big words, by it. I shall now claim my free drink from Mr Downes, which is the only payment I have been offered for this deathless prose

Simon Wolstencroft BA (HONS)
Editor, Publisher, and All-Round Good Guy
Tropical World Magazine
2006

Koi carp rising

A bright Koi rising
Mouth beaking my trailing hand;
Sun sparkling our touch,
No tension strains our surface
Our surface has no tension.

John Bailey

INTRODUCTION

> **Koi** are ornamental domesticated varieties of the common carp *Cyprinus carpio*, originated from China and widely spread in Japan. They are very closely related to goldfish, and in fact the style of breeding and ornamentation has become very similar, probably through the efforts of Japanese breeders to emulate goldfish, but they are not goldfish. Koi and tattoos of Koi are traditionally considered lucky.
>
> Wikipedia – *The Free Encyclopaedia*

Koi carp were certainly lucky for me. As anyone who has ever read my autobiography – *Monster Hunter* – will know, the beginning of the 21st Century was a particularly bleak time for me. Beset with health problems, I was also facing the threat of imminent bankruptcy. The Centre for Fortean Zoology [CFZ] was in the financial doldrums; it was costing an arm and a leg to keep going, and all of our regular sources of funding had dried up!

For years I have augmented my income by working as a `hack` writer, penning throwaway articles for anyone who will pay me. Regularly, I would get the bus into Exeter City Centre, and sneak into W.H. Smiths and peruse the magazines for sale, and make a surreptitious list of any new publications whom I could approach to buy an article from me.

One day in the late winter, I was doing just this when I found a copy of a magazine called *Koi Carp*. With my tongue firmly in cheek, I telephoned them, and asked whether they would be interested in an article – or even a series of articles – about the fortean aspects of their hobby. Much to my surprise and gratification they accepted, and so I started work on my first article.

I had been so used to working for fly-by-night publications, that I had stopped taking a long-term view of my writing work. I was lucky if a series I wrote lasted three issues, so the fact that I knew next to nothing about the fortean aspect of koi carp keeping didn't really matter. However, on this occasion, I was hoist by my own petard, as the series carried on for nearly two years! After six or seven issues, I bit the bullet, and started to employ the old journalistic adage that one should never let the truth get in the way of a good story.

Some of the stories that follow are true. Some are mostly true, others have a germ of truth, and even the ones that I made up are based on true events. I think my proudest moment as a journalist came, after the publication of "They Saved Hitler's Koi", when Simon Wolstencroft, an old friend of mine, and then editor of a sister-magazine to the one for which I was working, sent me the following email.

1. How did you think you would get away with having this printed?
2. How *did* you get away with it?

For goodness sake, don't read these stories looking for any firm insights into the history and culture of koi keeping, but I hope that they may give you some little amusement, because that was the spirit in which they were written.

Slainte mhor

Jonathan Downes,
The Centre for Fortean Zoology,
Woolfardisworthy,
North Devon

August 2006.

CHAPTER ONE
A NOBLE FISH

While a Chinese book of the Western Jin Dynasty (4th century) mentions carp with various colours, Koi breeding become popular in the 19th century in the Niigata prefecture of Japan. Farmers working the rice fields would notice that some carp would be more brightly coloured than others, capture them, and raise them (when normally the brighter colours would doom the fish to be more likely eaten by birds and other predators).

Wikipedia – *The Free Encyclopaedia*

Koi Carp are ancient and beautiful fish, and they have been kept as pets for many centuries. It is not surprising, therefore, that over the years many legends and an enormous amount of folklore has become associated with them. Probably because it has long been a nation of sailors and fishermen, Japanese culture is fascinated with rivers, lakes and the sea. It is not surprising therefore that fish, both marine and freshwater are extraordinarily important to the Japanese. Seafood has always been essential to the Japanese diet from ancient times and even today fish are still the main source of protein for the Japanese. It is hardly surprising, therefore, that so much of Japanese folklore and mythology is concerned with our piscine cousins.

However, the Japanese don't just eat fish, they pioneered the art of aquaculture and have been keeping our scaly friends for millennia. As the centuries passed various fish species began to assume mythic characteristics in the eyes of the Japanese. The Sea Bream or *Tai* for example is regarded as a good luck fish in Japan. Because of it is often served at weddings and other happy occasions.

Although Koi are ornamental fish rather than a food species, they too have a great deal of symbolism attached to them. Koi Carp are a symbol of strength, courage and patience. Somewhere along the line they have become confused with salmon, because it is popularly believed that they too `climb` up waterfalls to reach their spawning grounds and the phrase "**Koi no takinobori** (Koi's waterfall climbing)" means, "to succeed vigorously in life".

On the festival known as Children`s Day which falls on May 5th families with young boys fly *Koinobori* (carp streamers) outside their houses. These are stationary kites made of paper and cloth and decorated to look like stylised carp (although it has to be said that they look more like loaches!) As is so common amongst the religions of the orient, the devotees believe that these paper carp become `prayer flags` and that as they flutter in the brisk spring breezes they carry the wishes and prayers of those who made them to heaven. It is traditional for the parents of young boys to pray that their sons will grow as strong and brave as a Koi Carp.

It is rather touching to realise that at the beginning of the twenty first century citizens of one of the most powerful industrial nations on earth still believe in such a charming tradition (even if the zoology behind it is somewhat flawed). But it wasn't until I found that I had to write a column about these fish each month that I began exploring more aspects of the folklore (both ancient and modern) of Koi Carp and their relatives and discovering quite how peculiar the relationship between mankind and these beautiful fish has become.

Chapter Two
Enter the Dragon

The **dragon** is a mythical creature typically depicted as a large and powerful serpent or other reptile, with magical or spiritual qualities. Mythological creatures possessing some or most of the characteristics typically associated with dragons are common throughout the world's cultures.

Wikipedia – *The Free Encyclopaedia*

Every koi hobbyist and reader of this magazine will agree that the koi carp is a noble fish. Their grace and beauty has entranced generations of fishkeepers. But did you know that the earliest koi keepers truly believed that they were nurturing baby dragons?

Unlike the western image of a fire spewing, man eating, city destroying monster, the Oriental dragon is considered a benevolent creature. They were believed to control rainfall, the oceans and the weather. The breath of the eastern dragon condensed and formed rain although lightning was also believed to be dragons breath. If angered or treated with disrespect a dragon could cause a drought or flood. It could bring about an earthquake or send a tsunami crashing into coastal areas. Such acts of aggression were rare and generally the dragons of the east were mild in comparison to their western kin.

In China the dragon when through a complex staged life-cycle lasting 4000 years. Dragon eggs were believed to take 1000 years to hatch. The emergent dragon was tiny and limbless, resembling a water snake. Hence the proverb "Do not despise the snake because he has no horns. Who is to say he will no one day become a dragon?"

After a further 1000 years the dragon has reached its first major in-carnation. This is known as a *Kiao*. It is still snake like in shape but is of a vast size and has the head of a gigantic carp.

Over the next millennium the dragon grows a reptilian head and four clawed legs. Then it is known as a *Lung*. Five hundred years later branching horns spring forth from its head and the dragon enters the next stage of development as a *Kioh-lung.*

Finally a further millennium brings forth a pair of wings making the eastern dragon look like a slender, ornate version of the western dragon. In this its ultimate incarnation the mighty beast is called a *Ying-lung* or true dragon.

The dragon`s scales resemble those of a carp. The dragon`s resem-blance's are: The horns of a deer, the ears of a horse, the scales of a carp, the eyes of a daemon, the neck of a snake, the head of a camel, the paws of a tiger, and the claws of an eagle.

Carp who made it through the Lung men rapids in the third moon of each year become dragons. Hence the symbol of a carp struggling up the rapids on its way to become a dragon was adopted by scholars studying for office.

CHAPTER THREE
FAKIR FISH

Teleportation is the process of moving objects from one place to another more or less instantaneously, without passing through the intervening space. The word was coined in the early 1900's by American writer Charles Fort to describe the strange disappearances and appearances of anomalies, which he suggested may be connected. He joined the Greek prefix "tele-" (meaning "distant") to the latter part of the word "transportation".

Wikipedia – *The Free Encyclopaedia*

The word `teleport` has now become a familiar part of the English language due to television programmes like *Star Trek,* but did you know that the term was first coined nearly a century ago by the American Philosopher Charles Fort who has become the guru of those of us who spend our life studying unsolved mysteries? He came up with the concept to explain how some animals seem to be able to defy logic by turning up in areas where they could not possibly have arrived by any natural means.

This is a phenomenon that occurs throughout the natural world. The Queen of the Termite species *Macrotermes bellicosus* is so grotesquely huge that it is practically immobile. However, on innumerable occasions there have been reports of them disappearing from one tiny cell within the termite next only to reappear in a different one when the connecting corridors are plainly far too small to allow her to traverse through them.

∫TRENGTH THR☼UGH K☼I

The annals of fortean literature are full of stories of ponds and lakes, which though completely artificial, and which have never been stocked by their owners are nevertheless found, overnight, to be stocked with a healthy population of fish of various ages. However, one of the strangest stories that I have ever come across in my investigations into such things involved a Buddhist shrine near the Portuguese Consulate in the old sector of Victoria City in Hong Kong. This has probably long since been pulled down for redevelopment, but when I was a small boy in the early 1960s it was still a poignant reminder of a more gentle and relaxed age. The buildings were set in a small public garden, and when I was about five years old my Amah used to take me and my baby brother there for walks.

There was a huge, ornate, pond with a gothic stone fountain in the middle of it, and although to the best of my recollection the fountain never worked and the pond was always clogged with weed, it was the first time in my life that I ever saw Koi Carp. These magnificent fish swam lazily through the weedy water and entranced me, starting a love affair that has continued on and off ever since.

However, the strangest thing about these carp was that no-one knew where they had come from. The pond had been built at the beginning of the century, and the garden was one of the few parts of the city to have come through the Japanese dive-bombing strikes in 1941 relatively unscathed. After the war, naturalist G.A.K.Herklots was called to look at the pond. It hadn't been cleaned out since 1922, but there was no egress from any other body of water. Even then Victoria City was a fairly polluted area, and this tiny pond was a veritable oasis – probably the only piece of fresh, clean water for many miles.

The workmen cleaning out the pond were amazed at the amount of wildlife that had taken up residence there. There was a thriving family of Paradise Fish *(Macropodus opercularis)* several large freshwater crabs *(Potamon hongkongiensis)* and a large number of different freshwater shrimps. There were also the two large koi carp that I was to visit on occasion twenty years later.

Now, if one is prepared to suspend ones skepticism for a while one can imagine the crustacea arriving in egg form on the legs of visiting water birds. Possibly even the Paradise fish. It would seem highly unlikely but it would seem just about possible. But how did the koi carp get there? They were at least twenty years old, and no-one admitted responsibility for having placed them there. Devotees of Charlie Fort will no doubt immediately decide that they had teleported there by some strange biomechanical mechanism unknown to man. However I'm not too sure. I like to think that perhaps, some elderly Chinese fish keeper, realising that war was imminent, decided to place his beloved pets in the fountain hoping that somehow, the fact that it was adjacent to a shrine to the Lord Buddha – protector of all living things – would protect them from harm during the forthcoming conflict.

If this little fantasy of mine is true, then the old fishkeeper`s plan certainly worked, because when I last saw the fish, when I Hong Kong for the last time in 1980 they were still there. I hope that if, as I fear, the area has long since been modernised, the fish will have been moved to another safe haven, because as well as being magnificent creatures, they are an enduring childhood memory, and as such very dear to me.

Perhaps one of the readers of this little book can find out for me.

CHAPTER FOUR
ALL YOU NEED IS KOI

George Harold Harrison, MBE (24 February (not 25 February 1943 – 29 November 2001) was a popular English guitarist, singer, songwriter, record producer, and film producer, best known as a member of *The Beatles*. Harrison was the lead guitarist of *The Beatles*. During the band's extremely successful career, John Lennon and Paul McCartney were its main songwriters. However, Harrison usually wrote and sang lead on one or two songs per album which earned him growing admiration as a considerable talent in his own respect.

Wikipedia – *The Free Encyclopaedia*

Once upon a time, (as all the best stories begin), about ten or fifteen years ago, I was wandering across Dartmoor with my dog Toby (now sadly deceased). Toby was quite a young dog then, and the ravages of middle age which have somewhat curtailed my mobility in recent years, had not taken their toll, and so the two of us were quite a long way from the nearest road.

I have always been a keen amateur naturalist and for over thirty years I have been exploring the wilds of Dartmoor in search of its more elusive wildlife. Now, I'm not going to tell you exactly where we were for reasons that shall become obvious, but Toby and I were heading for some remote quarries where, after having read an obscure 19th Century booklet about the area, we had been led to believe that there might be a colony of great crested newts.

∫TRENGTH THR⊕VGH K⊕I

For such an apparently desolate locality, Dartmoor has been inhabited for an awfully long time, and there are strange deserted rock workings and quarries all over the moor. One of the most famous if about half a mile from the famous tourist beauty spot of Haytor, and as well as a thriving colony of palmated newts supports a small but apparently healthy population of wild goldfish! I suppose that I should not have been surprised therefore to find that when, eventually, Toby and I reached our destination, although there were no Great Crested Newts to be seen, there were at least a dozen, enormous koi carp of various colours swimming lazily backwards and forwards in the dark blue water.

To say that I was flabbergasted would be somewhat of an understatement. Goldfish in a relatively accessible pond within half a mile of a main road I could understand. But koi? And furthermore, koi of various colours swimming perfectly at home in a flooded quarry so remote that it had taken over three hours of hard walking to get there. Although I know exactly where to go, I am sure that I would not physically be able to get there any more.

Although the quarry is marked on the ordinance survey maps, it is so remote that I can imagine that it is quite likely that no-one visits it from one year's end to another, so as far as I know the koi are still there. This is why I have no intention of revealing the location, because by my reckoning there is well over a grand`s worth of fish swimming around in the quarry. But how on earth did they get there?

On my return to Exeter I quietly tried to investigate the matter. Could there, I wondered, once have been a large house in the area? All over Devonshire one can find isolated patches of rhododendron woodland, which upon investigation mark the sites where, a couple of centuries ago there was once the home of a minor member of the local gentry. If the gentry could leave their herbaceous borders behind, could they not have done the same with their fish?

However, my researches led me to the conclusion that there was no house in the immediate vicinity, and furthermore, there never had been!

However, an old 19th Century photograph of the quarry showed a small stone hut built precariously into the rock face at the edge of the pool. There was no mention of anyone having lived there and I could only imagine that it had been the home of one of the blasters or quarrymen who could have originally constructed the quarry, many years before it had become deserted and filled with water. The problem remained a nagging one at the back of my mind for years until just before last Christmas when an elderly hippy mate of mine came to join me in a Christmas noggin of brandy. We were drinking to the memory of the late George Harrison – the guitarist of the *Beatles*, who had died at the end of November, when he gave me a piece of information which in one fell swoop may have solved the mystery once and for all.

Back in 1967 and 1968, many of the rock music illuminati including George Harrison, Mick Jagger and Brian Jones became interested in eastern mysticism and also in the study of UFOs. Several of these famous musicians including (or so I am told Harrison) were involved with several organisations who would go to remote parts of the west-country to sit out in the dark and look for flying saucers. They felt that the occupants would be able to impart amazing pearls of wisdom to them about the nature of the universe.

One of the places where these famous skywatchers would congregate, so my friend told me, were various quarries and tors on the western edge of Dartmoor. A few days later he took me to a secret place in Holne Chase woods where various hippy luminaries had made a Japanese Garden deep in the woods in order to meditate as they waited for the extra-terrestrials. Surely, he suggested, it was not beyond the bounds of possibility that someone, quite possibly `the quiet Beatle` had done the same thing in my quarry in the middle of Dartmoor.

It made perfect sense to me. However this made me even more determined not to reveal where these beautiful fish are living. With the death of both Harrison and Lennon, *Beatles* memorabilia is reaching ridiculous prices at auction. If a pair of Ringo`s drum sticks reaches nearly five figures, how much would someone pay for George Harison`s pet fish?

If indeed the gentle and spiritual man who I had met once, and whose simple spirituality had touched the lives of tens of thousands of people, had stocked this remote pond with rare and beautiful koi, they should stay there as a rare gift to delight the intrepid traveller who stumbles across them. They shouldn`t end up in an auction room, or worse stuffed in a glass case.

So I ain`t telling you where they are.

Hare Bol George.

CHAPTER FIVE
METHUSELAH`S CHILDREN

Methuselah's Children is a 1941 science fiction novel by Robert A. Heinlein, originally serialised in *Astounding Science Fiction* (July, August, September 1941). It was expanded into a full-length novel in 1958. Heinlein used his "Future History" series of stories (*The Man Who Sold the Moon, Revolt in 2100*, etc.) as a background for this novel about the long-lived Howard Families, star travel, and human freedom.

Wikipedia – *The Free Encyclopaedia*

"...and all the days of Methuselah were nine hundred and sixty nine years and he died"
Genesis Ch 5 v 27

If you ask any expert on the subject of koi carp, they will tell you that if they are properly looked after, these fish can live between seventy and a hundred years. This is a generally accepted zoological truism and ties in with what we know about the longevity of various other freshwater fish species such as sturgeon and European catfish (wels). However, it has been claimed by some very reputable, (and as we shall see, some fairly disreputable) sources, that these magnificent fish can, in fact live for much much longer.

As far back as 1974, koi expert Takehiko Tamak claimed in his book *Nishikigoi Fancy Koi,* that one specimen had proved to be at least 222 years old in 1973, and that this extraordinary age was determined by counting the scale rings by electron microscope. A friend of mine – a zoologist working at Southampton University - told me recently that some people even believe that the extra large specimens found in some of the sacred temple pools in remote parts of Japan may be over a thousand years old. After all they have been cared for more diligently than any other fish on the planet.

This is where it starts to get creepy.

A series of books by science fiction author Robert A Heinlein, describe mankind`s search for the cure for senescence (ageing). Heinlein happens to be my favourite author, and I have often vaguely wondered whether his literary speculations have been mirrored in the real world. Apparently they have, and according to some sources, the fish that koi devotees lavish their care, attention and income upon may be at the centre of this real life quest for Methuselah`s children.

Like mammals, fish display patterns of rapid and gradual senescence, such as the Pacific salmon and Medaka, respectively. But unlike warm-blooded animals, some poikilotherms exhibit negligible senescence, which is chronological aging without an increase in mortality rate. Zoologist Leonard Hayflick, writing twenty years after Takehiko Tamak observed that *"If they do age, it occurs at such a slow rate that their aging has not been demonstrated convincingly"*, and he felt that this phenomenon was an important avenue to study.

Nearly a decade later we are (officially at least) no nearer the answer. Since fish with gradual senescence exhibit a decline in reproductive capacity, oxidative metabolism, protein utilisation and cell numbers it seems certain that the lowered metabolism of cold-blooded animals alone cannot be the answer. If this were true then all poikilothermic creatures would live longer than us poor fragile endotherms and this certainly ain`t the case. Some species of fish, after all, live their entire reproductive cycle in a matter of months. Therefore, to quote from an article called *"Ageing in Cold-Blooded Vertebrates"*, published in the *International Journal of Experimental and Clinical Gerontology,* V40, 1994):

"information derived on the mechanism causing extended longevity in such species might be useful in finding clues for life extension strategies in humans"

As well as my work as a zoologist, I have written a number of books about UFOs. I have always tried to approach the subject from a scientific point of view because I believe that 90% (if not more) of what is written about the subject is complete bosh. However, books on UFOl-

ogy sell more than books on the more obscure aspects of exotic zoology, and I have a mortgage to pay, a fiancee to keep happy, and a
houseful of exotic animals to feed. As a result of these books I have
become a fairly regular fixture on the UFO Conference and lecture cir-
cuit both in the UK and in America.

It was at a recent conference in Nevada, when I received the last
piece of information which is pertinent to this article. I was sitting at
dinner (OK I was in the bar, but who is quibbling), talking to some fel-
low delegates, and as is so often the case we were talking about absolutely anything EXCEPT for the subject of UFOs. The subject drifted
onto fishkeeping and we began to discuss, Takehiko Tamak`s claims.

Anyone with even the slightest knowledge of UFOs will have heard of
the rumours that the secret Airforce bases at Area 51 in Nevada and
at Rudloe Manor in Salisbury Plain are not only the sites for secret
government experiments involving back-engineering alien technology
salvaged from crashed flying saucers, but are even the places where
aliens (either living or dead) which have been taken from the afore-
mentioned UFO crashes are kept.

Now, for the record, I would like to say that although I will not cate-
gorically state that there is *no* intelligent life anywhere outside this
planet. I think that it is highly unlikely that there are pickled aliens in
jars hidden in secret caverns deep beneath the Nevada desert, or the
Wiltshire countryside. However there is no doubt that these places ex-
ist, and it seems almost certain that secret scientific projects are un-
dertaken at both locations. A colleague, who was sitting at the bar
with me that night in Nevada, claimed that his brother was one of the
foremost fish dealers in the state. (I later checked this claim and
found it to be true). He furthermore claimed that the US Government
had a long standing contract to provide regular shipments of koi carp
to the base. On my return to the UK, I did a little covert detective
work of my own, and found that another well known koi supplier in the
south of England was making regular shipments to Rudloe Manor.

Now, we are left with a number of possibilities. Either the powers that
be are bilaterally deciding to keep a well stocked koi pond at each military base, so that the lonely servicemen stationed there can follow in
the spiritual footsteps of generations of Shinto monks, and meditate
on the relaxing joy of these huge and contemplative fishes, or something else is afoot. Could Governments on both sides of the Atlantic be
researching ways of ensuring that people could live longer? Is this
what the hapless koi carp are being used for? If this is true then they
would have to keep this a secret. There are too many people living on
this tiny planet as it is. Longevity treatment could only be used by the
scientific, social and political elite otherwise the planet would soon be-

come completely untenable...

[AUTHOR`S NOTE: I finished writing this article late in the evening on the 1st February. In *The Observer* on the 3rd February was a fascinating artcle which began:

"Scientists have pinpointed the Methuselah gene - a stretch of DNA that confers healthy old age on men and women - raising the prospect that researchers may one day be able to create drugs that extend human life......"

I wonder whether our favourite fish species was responsible for this scientific breakthrough?]

Live long and prosper dudes....

CHAPTER SIX
THE GREAT KOI KAPER

Loch Ness (Scottish Gaelic: *Loch Nis*) is a large, deep freshwater loch in the Scottish Highlands (57°18′N 4°27′W) extending for approximately 37 km (23 miles) southwest of Inverness. The Loch's surface is 15.8 metres above sea level.. Loch Ness is best known for the alleged sightings of the legendary Loch Ness Monster ("Nessie"), although it is scenic in its own right. Boat cruises operate from various locations along its shores giving tourists the chance to look for the monster.

Wikipedia – *The Free Encyclopaedia*

During my long and chequered career as an investigator into the weird and wonderful, it will not, I am sure, surprise regular readers of this column to discover that I have visited Loch Ness. Indeed the dark waters which fill the Great Glen have held an irresistible fascination for me since I was a small boy. Everyone has heard of Nessie – the huge, long-necked beastie which is said to lurk in the murky peat stained waters, but there are other mysteries and strange stories to be told about the area. For example:

- A strange leathery bird-like creature called the *boobrie* has been seen on occasion flapping slowly across the landscape.
- The notorious black magician Aleister Crowley once lived in Boleskine House on the shores of the geat lake
- Mystery cats have been seen in the vicinity

STRENGTH THR◉UGH K◉I

And

- Legendary Loch Ness researcher Ted Holiday was so convinced that parts of the lake contained a great evil of Lovecraftian proportions that he persuaded Rev Donald Ormond to exorcise the lake of evil demons.

However none of these terrifying tales hold a candle to the bizarre tale of mystery that I have called *The Great Koi Kaper of Loch Ness.*

One day about ten years ago during one of my monster hunting visits to Scotland I was in a pub in one of the lochside hamlets when I got talking to a rather shifty looking Londoner called Charlie. Much to my surprise, it turned out that Charlie wasn't, like me, a *sassenach* on a monster hunting expedition, but that he had moved up to Loch Ness several years before with his family, and was an employee of the local water company. He hated it up there, and longed for his native flesh-pots of the South East, but, he said, he could never return. He was trapped up there for the rest of his life!

As you do.. we got talking about the monster, and I expressed the opinion that some sightings, especially those which had taken place on land, could have been of otters. Although most specimens of the European otter (*Lutra lutra*) are only a few feet long, specimens measuring up to six feet in length have been shot, and in Ireland there are legends of a creature called the *Dobhar Chu* or master otter which is supposed to grow even bigger.

"Don´t talk to me about bleeding otters" said my new friend, with far more venom than I could ever have imagined the subject warranting. *"It was bleeding otters that stopped me making my bleeding fortune"....*

Well, an opening conversational gambit like that could not be ignored, and I had to know more, so I bought Charlie a pint of Tennants 80 Shillings, and a malt whisky chaser and sat back to enjoy his story.

It all began when one of Charlie`s colleagues had been visiting a garden centre which sold koi carp as a sideline. He was immediately entranced not just by the ancient beauty of these gorgeous and majestic fish but for the fact that some of them were going for prices of up to a grand. He told Charlie about it. "`*ere, I want a bit of that"* he thought elegantly, and the two of them began to hatch a cunning plan.

They were both water board employees and the huge water tanks of which they were joint custodians, would, they thought make fine rearing vats for koi carp. Wouldn`t it be a wizard wheeze to buy lots of small fish at a couple of quid, and rear them in these giant, secluded stone vats where nobody else ever went, and then flog them for a grand apeice?

However, a quick visit to the library soon disillusioned them of this idea. As soon as they realised the length of time it would take for a two quid koi to turn into one worth a grand, they gave up on it, but they soon came up with a bigger, better, and far more nefarious scheme. Charlie had a brother-in-law called `Big Paul` who lived in one of the less salubrious suburbs of Harlow New Town. `Big Paul` was usually described by his associates as being a *"Diamond Geezer"*, but from what I could gather from talking to his brother-in-law, he was a rather unpleasant thug and petty criminal, whose stock in trade were *"dodgy motahs"* and *"bent MOTs"* but who was not averse to the odd bit of petty thievery on the side.

Whereas garden centres that sell koi carp are few and far between in the Scottish Highlands, they are two a penny in Essex, and between them Charlie and Big Paul started to plan a commando style raid on one of the more secluded Essex Garden Centres. The idea was to steal about thirty thousand pounds worth of koi carp, and rush them in `Big Paul`s` van up to Inverness where they could be released into the water board ponds where they could be kept in seclusion until they were fenced on with forged paperwork to unsuspecting customers. `Big Paul`, Charlie, and Charlie`s un-named "mate" looked likely to net a cool ten grand each out of the operation.

The raid went ahead like clockwork. It had been planned with military precision, and was carried out in a fashion which would have made the SAS proud. Charlie and `Big Paul` then drove hell for leather up the M1 towards Scotland. By the time that they reached the secluded water treatment works in the hills above Loch Ness, it was the following morning, and they were exhausted. However they still had one task to do. Taking the big plastic containers that they had brought especially for their precious cargo, they carefully carried each one to the side of the great stone basin, where they took the lid off and tipped the enormous fish into the water.

After the whole of their ill gotten gains had been liberated, Charlie and Big Paul sat back, lit cigarettes and surveyed their swimming swag with a feeling of a job well done. However, theirs were not the only eyes watching the great red and gold fish.

"So what happened?" I asked. *"Did you get away with it? Did your employers find out?"*

Charlie grimaced at me *"They didn`t get a bleeding chance. There* were thirty five fish in that storage tank, and within a week they were all gone."

I looked at him quizzically and would have raised one eyebrow if it wasn't for the fact that although it looks incredibly cool I have never been able to do it.

"It was the bleeding otters" he said "They ate the bleeding lot. Thirty bleeding grand's worth of the bleeders".....

I started to laugh uncontrollably. Although I was sorry that the noble fish had met such an ignominious end the whole affair had an irresistibly comic side to it. I was laughing so hard that I almost missed what Charlie had to say next....

"....and that's why I'm stuck here in the bleeding north of Scotland, because 'Big Paul 'says if I ever come back to Harlow without his ten grand, he'll bleeding have my kneecaps".

Realising that a platitude about crime not paying would not really be appropriate at this stage, I bought Charlie another beer, and went out into the gathering Inverness dusk in search of the monster....

CHAPTER SEVEN
A FISHY ROMANCE

Katsushika Hokusai (1760-1849) was an Edo period Japanese artist, painter, wood engraver and ukiyo-e maker, born in Edo (now Tokyo). Author of the 13-volume sketchbook *Hokusai manga* (begun in 1814) and the block prints *Thirty-six Views of Mount Fuji*, (created around 1823-1829), which includes "In the Hollow of a Wave off the Coast at Kanagawa."

Wikipedia – *The Free Encyclopaedia*

Possibly the greatest challenge that faced me in my career writing for *Koi Carp*, was how to present this particular instalment of *Kurious Koi* in a tasteful manner fit for a family magazine edited by a charming young lady. As anyone who has ever seen my abode will know, that wherever you go in my little house there are books. Thousands and thousands of them. My library covers a range of esoteric and unlikely subjects, from the academic to the bizarre, and from the wholesome to the rather sordid.

One of the more peculiar books in my collection is by a Dutch writer called Midas Dekker. The book, *Dearest Pet* explores the history of, erm - how do I put it - "the intimate liaisons" of human beings throughout history who have chosen to lavish their affections in a physical manner upon a partner of a different species.

From the point of view of a cryptozoolgist like me this is quite an interesting subject because the book is an academic one which, amongst

Katsushika Hokusai (葛飾北斎) (1760 - 1849)
The Dream of the Fisherman's Wife

other things covers the legends, that imply that entities such as the hairy wild men and satyrs of Greek and Roman legend (the Bigfoot of the ancient world if you like) were the result of liaisons between people and wild beasts.

Tucked on page 154 is an extraordinary engraving, attributed to a 19th Century Japanese artist called Kastushika Hokusai which shows, in graphic detail an attractive young woman in an amorous clinch with an octopus. It is a striking, disturbing and peculiar image, but unfortunately the book tells us nothing about it. I was mildly interested, because the same picture also features what seems to be a giant squid. To find a picture of a giant squid – one of the most enigmatic creatures in the world - in a piece of 19th Century Japanese pornography intrigued me and I wanted to find out more.

A friend of mine belongs to the Anglo-Japanese Friendship Society, and so I showed him the picture. He was amazed and slightly shocked, but promised that he would find out as much as he could about the provenance of the picture and the story behind it. A week later he telephoned me with an extraordinary little folk-tale which I am reproducing pretty well as he told it to me.

Once upon a time in Ancient Japan the Emperor had a beautiful daughter. She had many suitors but the Emperor was a very stern and exacting father and he believed that none of the young princelings and brave samurai who courted his daughter were worthy of her. However, it seems that the young princess was somewhat of a flibbertigibbet, and so to protect her virtue, the Emperor built a small house for her on one of the small and virtually uninhabited islands off the coast of Japan. The little house was in the middle of a beautiful garden with a stream running through it. He then built a tall wall around the garden and locked the gate so that no-one could leave or enter without his permission.

However, just down the coast from the princess's prison there was a little fishing village in which lived an adventurous young man who heard about the princess's predicament. One early morning he crept out of his parent's house and journeyed up the river to the wall of the garden but it was guarded by the fiercest and most savage warriors of the kingdom. However, he managed to climb a tree and sneak a look over the high wall.

What he saw astounded him. The young princess – famed far and wide as the most beautiful young woman of all Japan – was performing her ablutions in a state of undress in the river. After just one look at the naked princess the young fisherboy fell in love with her and made a vow to the God of the Sea (his own particular pet deity, unsurprisingly because of his profession) that he would make her his wife at any cost.

If copping a sneaky look at a naked royal chick wasn`t risky enough when she was guarded by a bevy of heavily armed soldiers, his next act was positively stupid. He entreated the previously mentioned Sea God for his aid. Now, as anyone who has ever read fairy tales will know, asking a deity for help with matters of the heart and loins is a risky business. The deity will often accede to the request, but will usually do something nasty in return. This case was no different.

The mighty God of the Sea appeared before him in a flash of smoke, or whatever it is happens when a Deity of the Deep appears to an illiterate fisherboy, and after a bit of argument agreed to help him. The boy promised that if the Sea God would provide a way for the boy to enter the walled garden, and if, when he had done so the princess would not only fall in love with him but allow him to seduce her, then he [the fisherboy] would be the servant of the Sea God forever, in whatever capacity the Sea God chose. This was, as events turned out, not a good idea.

The Sea God snapped his seaweedy fingers, and turned the boy into a large, beautiful, golden fish with little barbels around his mouth, such as had never been seen before in Japan (or indeed anywhere else), and in his fishy form, the young fisherboy swam under the wall, up the river and into the walled garden, where the Princess was still swimming, naked under the warm Japanese sun.

Now, as previously mentioned, the Princess was an amorous young flibbertigibbet and was becoming tired of her solitary state. When she spied this magnificent fish, nearly the size of her whole body she had a very naughty [and somewhat unsavoury idea]. Her father, the Emperor had strictly forbidden her to slake her lust on any of her suitors, and as she was, on the whole at least an obedient daughter she had obeyed him. However, she reasoned to herself with the amazing capacity for self delusion that so many women have when it comes to affairs of the heart, her father could not have meant that her object of desire could not be a large and splendid fish.

She approached the fish with open arms, and the young fisherboy, not believing his luck, swam towards her. As they kissed the young fisherboy regained his human form, and as she looked into his eyes they fell deeply and irrevocably in love. They then consummated their passion in the usual manner and as they lay blissfully on the grass, in rushed the Emperor together with his posse of soldiers.

He was understandably upset, and summarily condemned the young couple to death. They were just about to be killed in nasty ways, when the Sea God, who was quite a kindly old geezer despite his habit of sending Tsunamis to destroy coastal villages reappeared on the scene. He argued that a *God* outclassed even an Emperor, pulled rank, and interceded with the cruel monarch; persuading him not to kill his daughter and son-in-law. In return he promised that he would take the young fisherboy into his service, and that neither the Emperor or his daughter would see him again.

He turned to the young fisherboy and told him that from henceforth he would be a general in the Sea God`s Army and he turned him into a Giant Squid – the most fearsome creature of the sea. Upon hearing this tragic news, both the princess and the squid burst into tears, and fell into each others arms/tentacles. The Emperor and the Sea God relented slightly, and said that the squid could return home for conjugal visits once a year. This mollified the heartbroken young lovers slightly, and so whilst the Sea God and the newly created Giant Squid swam out to sea to do their own inimitable thing, the young princess, now pregnant, sat back in her walled prison to await her lover`s return a year later.

When the squid returned to his wife a year later (the event illustrated in the etching by Kastushika Hokusai), it was to find out that he was a father. His wife had given birth to twins. His daughter was to be the mother of all the mermaids, and his son, a magnificent golden fish, was to be the father of all the koi carp. In a rather unsatisfactory sort of way, as far as I know, they all lived happily ever after.

This is why, to this day Giant Squid are seen off the coast of Japan only about once a year, and why koi carp are prized as royal fish. As far as the princess goes, somewhere off the coast of Japan there is a tiny island with a walled garden on it, and as far as I know….she is still there.

CHAPTER EIGHT
PHANTOM PHISH

A **morris dance** is a form of folk dance. There are English records mentioning the morris dance dating back to 1448, though dances with similar names and some similar features are mentioned in Renaissance documents in France, Italy, and Spain. The origins of the term are uncertain, but one of the most widely accepted theories is that the term was "moorish dance" and "Moresco" (in Spain), which was gradually corrupted to "morris dance". Another, perhaps simpler, explanation is that "Morris" comes from the Latin "Mores", meaning "a custom". This is consistent with the word (with various archaic spellings) sometimes being used to describe some other folk customs such as folk plays.

Wikipedia – *The Free Encyclopaedia*

I believe that it was Mr Ripley – the bloke who started the "believe it or not" newspaper columns in the 1950s, who first coined the phrase that `truth is stranger than fiction`. Too damn right it is! I have been scraping a living from the popular and academic press for well over a decade now by recounting true tales of high strangeness, that are far more bizarre than any story that Hollywood could devise.

One great example is Richard Gere`s recent Hollywood blockbuster *"The Mothman Prophecies"* which, although based vaguely on a true book by author John Keel, had to cut out all the weirdest parts of the book because *"The movie-going public simply wouldn`t believe them"*. I wonder if they are going to get Richard Gere to play me when they make the movie of the astounding true

ЅTRENᴳTH THR◉UᴳH K◉I

STORY OF THE GHOSTLY KOI CARP OF CHIPPING NORTON!

This all happened last summer (2001) while I was in the Cotswolds, pursuing my legitimate trade as a journalist writing up a story about a Cotswold`s Morris Dance festival. In the Beer Tent I got chatting to a lady "of a certain age" about life, the universe and everything, and the subject soon got on to my career as a paranormal journalist.

"You're not going to believe this" she told me, *"but I'm haunted ---- or at least the pond in my garden is".* I have to admit that at this point I was only half listening to her. I was too busy trying to wangle the conversation around to whether she was single or not, because she was a cute little thing, and a day of cheap beer and Morris Dancing as a spectator sport tends to make a middle aged journalist veer towards the amorous. However, her next words shocked me back both to reality and into my persona as a professional. *"yeah"* she told me *"my garden pond is haunted by the ghost of a koi carp that I had as a child".*

Well, I've always been interested in animal ghosts, because they seem to be of two main types:

1. Those which are attached to a particular person
2. Those which are attached to a particular place

And this one seemed to be a bit of both, so I eagerly asked her for more details.

Apparently, she lived in a big house on the outskirts of town, in which she had lived as a little girl. *"I moved away from home when I went to Uni, and then I got married"* she said *"but after the divorce and the kids had left home I moved back with my Mum, and when she died, I inherited the house, and I've lived there by myself ever since…."*

Apparently, only a few days after her mother had died, she was sitting reflectively by the garden pond when she saw a flash of gold and white in the water. This was strange, she thought, because although the pond was full of tadpoles, water beetles and newts, there were no fish of any kind there – and hadn't been for well over thirty years. But there it was again – the unmistakeable flash of a huge koi carp frolicking in the murky green waters.

And then it all came flooding back. *"Neptuuuuune!!!!"* she wailed, and burst into tears.

STRENGTH THROUGH KOI

She was visibly upset by this time, so I did what any gentleman would do, and offered to escort her home. She gratefully agreed, and so I telephoned for a taxi, and about twenty minutes later we were sitting together on a wrought iron bench by the side of her garden pond, drinking chardonnay, and staring into the stagnant depths before us.

She resumed the story, and with only the minimum of prompting from me, told me how, in 1963, when she had been only four years old, her late father had given her a large koi carp for her birthday present. Overjoyed with her new pet she, had christened him `Neptune`, and installed him in the very same pond that we were sitting beside thirty eight years later. Every day she would visit her pet, and apparently, he became quite tame, and would swim up to the mossy edge of the pond where she would feed him titbits of food.

Then, six months into their relationship disaster struck in the shape of the all pervading blight of Walt Disney! Apparently, she had been watching a cartoon featuring a talking fish who happened (with tragic serendipity) to have the same colouration as `Neptune`. As he talked – brightly coloured bubbles came out of his mouth. It just wasn't fair, she thought, that her beloved Neptune couldn't make bubbles like that, so her four year old mind started working overtime.

Unfortunately for `Neptune`, the same birthday which had seen her acquire him, had seen her being given a plastic toy fish (about the same size and shape as `Neptune`) which was filled with Bubble Bath. Being an intelligent little four-year-old, (but knowing next to nothing about piscine physiology) she decided that if she poured the entire stock of bubble bath into the pond She was sure that once he had acclimatised, `Neptune` would be breathing beautiful, multi-coloured bubbles...and you never know, she thought, the bubbles might even be the magickal link that would make her beloved pet fish be able to talk to her, just like the cartoon fish she had seen on television.

She went to bed that night excited and happy, and her dreams were full of the wonderful adventures she was going to have the next day with `Neptune`, her magickal talking fish. She woke up at first light the next morning and went rushing out to the pond to say good morning to `Neptune`, hoping against hope that he might be able to talk back to her...

No-one reading this magazine will be surprised to hear that all she found was the fishpond covered in a nasty chemical goo, and there, floating belly up in the middle of the pond was `Neptune`. Dead as a doornail.
"I was inconsolable" she told me with tears in her eyes. *"I cried for days and days, and even when I stopped crying, I promised myself*

that I would never have another pet fish, and that there would never be any more fish in the pond, and there never have been!"

She was visibly upset, and I put my arm around her shoulders to comfort her. Through her tears she pointed to a little gravestone set under a lilac bush in the far corner of the garden. *"I still put flowers on his grave even now…"* she sobbed.

My personal interpretation of events, was that the death of her pet had been an enormous emotional trauma to the young girl, and when, three and a bit decades later her mother had died leaving her totally alone in the world, this second emotional trauma had somehow triggered the memories of her childhood, and created (in her mind at least) a phantasm of her beloved pet, for whose death she still felt an intolerable guilt.

However, this ain't the sort of thing that you tell a grieving woman, (especially a cute one), who has managed to fool herself that the ghost of her pet fish is somehow haunting her. I wasn't sure what to do. I may be a member of `Her Majesty's Press`, but I *do* have scruples, and one of them forbids me making a move on a woman who has asked me for help in dealing with grieving not only for her mother but for her pet fish.

Then she looked straight at me, shrieked with astonishment and threw her arms around my neck. *"You're the man who went to that island looking for Vampires – I've read your book – you can help me"* and she rushed off into the house, returning with a battered copy of my book *Only Fools and Goatsuckers* (2001) which tells the story of my adventures in Puerto Rico and Mexico hunting vampires with a Channel 4 TV crew. She hurriedly leafed through it until she found a passage describing my involvement in a ritual cobbled together from Celtic Magick and *Santeria* to dispel a vampire in the middle of the Mexican Desert. Well, the truth is, that most of that was done purely for the TV Cameras, and what little was left was directed at a malevolent vampiric entity called *el chupacabra*, rather than to get rid of a harmless phantom fish, which even if it had any objective reality whatsoever, was about as un-malevolent and un-vampiric as you can get.

I tried to explain this to the excited woman, but she wouldn't have any of it. Would I, she asked me, carry out an exorcism of her garden pond/ Of all the crazy things I have been asked to do in my long and chequered career, this was probably the craziest. Was I going to perform an exorcism? Of course not! For one thing there was nothing to exorcise, and for another I'm not, and never have been an exorcist. Was I going to perform some made up *Santeria* ritual full of hocus pocus just to make her happy? Possibly. It could do no possible harm, and might just put her mind at rest. But there was one other thing I wanted to try first.

I put my hand on her shoulder to calm her down. *"Have you thought, my dear"* I started in my most avuncular manner, *"that if `Neptune`s` ghost IS still here, he has come back to be a comfort to you in your hour of need. That he loved you as much as you loved him and that he is trying to be as supportive as the ghost of a long dead fish can be?"*

At this, she started to smile. *"I hadn't thought of that"* she said happily. *"But I tell you what I will do"* I continued, *"I will do something to make him go away, if he wants to and only stay if he wants to be with you as a fishy friend"*...

I couldn't believe I was saying this stuff, but needs must, and we walked hand in hand over to `Neptune's` grave, where I recited as much as I could remember of the Latin *Mass for the Dead* (which wasn't very much as I am a *very* lapsed Catholic), and added some made up bits of my own, and ceremoniously laid `Neptune's` soul to rest, thirty-seven years after his unfortunate demise.

By this time I was gasping for a pint, and so in the best tradition of the English journalist, I made my excuses and left. However, before doing so, I made a date to meet up with her for dinner the following evening.

The next night she was warm, happy and at ease. She had spent the rest of the evening (she said) chatting happily to `Neptune's` ghost as he gambolled fishily in the murky green waters. We had a wonderful meal with a lovely bottle of wine, and then we went back to her house for coffee. And by the way, just in case any of you want to know what happened next, you may well ask, but as a gentleman I couldn't *possibly* comment.

CHAPTER NINE
"OH MY GOD,
THEY'VE KILLED KENNEDY"

Kennedy was assassinated on November 22, 1963. Official investigations later determined Lee Harvey Oswald to be the culprit. His assassination is considered a defining moment in U.S. history due to its traumatic impact on the nation, its impact on the political history of the ensuing decades, his subsequent branding as an icon for a new generation of Americans and American aspirations, and for the mystery and conspiracy allegations that surround it.

Wikipedia – *The Free Encyclopaedia*

My mother died at the end of March 2002. She was 80 years old, and had been ill for many years, so it wasn't really a surprise, although her death leaves a gaping void in my life. From her I got a number of gifts that have been invaluable to me over the years. She gave me a love of books, a love of animals, and also my sense of the absurd. She also, in a roundabout way, gave me the story for this month's column.

A few issues ago I told you the story of how, when I was a little boy in Hong Kong, my amah (who was called Ah Tim), used to take me for a walk to an ornate pond, which was part of a Buddhist shrine near the

ſTRENCTH THRОVСH KОI

Portuguese Consulate in the old sector of Victoria City. During my mother's last illness, I sent her a photocopy of this story to amuse her as she was lying in her hospital bed. When we next spoke she reminded me of another koi-related story from my childhood.

During the Colonial twilight of the mid 1960s, my mother was a member of a venerable institution called The Ladies' Recreation Club (LRC). It was there she played tennis and had morning coffee with her friends, and where - amongst other things - I learned to swim. It was exactly what the name implied; a social and sports club for the wives of Colonial Service Officers. I had assumed that, like so many other relics of Hong Kong's Imperial past, the LRC would have been swept away on the surging tides of progress. However, as I sat at my computer writing on a balmy Sunday afternoon in 2002, I entered the name into my Internet Search Engine, and there it was

If you look at the picture on the front page of their website, you will see a patio just above the swimming pool. Back in the 1960s it boasted two large tanks containing koi carp. During the summer term, the weather in Hong Kong was so hot that primary school children used to start school an hour or so earlier in the mornings, and have the afternoons off. Invariably at least three afternoons a week, my mother would take my little brother and me down to the LRC to swim, whilst she would spend the afternoon chatting to her friends.

One of these friends was a terribly fierce-looking American lady called Mrs Ingersoll whose husband had been something to do with the Kennedy Administration. I was always terrified of her, because she was tall and thin, with blue rinsed hair, a hooked nose, *pince nez* glasses and a distinct aroma of gin. However, being a well brought up lad I was always polite, and when we met up at the LRC, she would take me by the hand over to the enormous tanks which held the lugubrious looking koi carp and tell me, in a miasma of gin fumes how Mr. Kennedy/Mr. President/ "Her darling John" (depending on how drunk she was) had adored koi, and how they could have saved him. I was only four years old when President Kennedy was shot, and was far too young to know what the fuss was about, but I know now that for many people it was the defining moment of the 1960s.

I had no idea who President Kennedy was, and at the time my only motivation was to get away from this horrible alcoholic woman, and back into the swimming pool, so I didn't really pay much attention to the story. At the time I vaguely assumed she was trying to say that if the President had kept fish instead of being President, he wouldn't have been killed, but even for an eight year old this didn't make much

The Texas Book Depository (top)
and The Grassy Knoll (bottom)

sense. I have since vaguely wondered whether Kennedy ever had fishponds, either at his private residence or at the White House. Flushed by my success in locating the website for the LRC, I chased around the Internet trying to get information about whether there was, indeed, a pond full of koi carp at the Presidential Official Residence - but to no avail. I therefore did what I always do when my avenues of research come to a sudden halt - I telephoned Nick Redfern.

Nick is an old mate of mine who is the author of several best selling books on UFOs and conspiracy theories. He lived an uneventful life in the west Midlands where dressed in black with a shaven head, he listened to punk music and investigated UFOs, until much to everyone's surprise he met a beautiful Texan lady, upped roots and disappeared off to live near Houston. We still keep in touch on a regular basis, and help each other out with our researches. He wasn't at all surprised to have me telephone in the small hours to talk about koi carp. Much to my surprise he burst out laughing. *"I've got something that you can use,"* he chuckled down the phone, *"God knows if it's got anything to do with your story, but it's a connection between JFK and koi carp."*

Ten minutes later I got the following e-mail:

Jon, here is the info on Agent Koi. This story is very little known even in JFK assassination circles. I don't know why he/she uses that name, maybe the story is 'fishy' or, like a koi, keeps getting bigger. But anyway this is the story.

Agent Koi worked in US Army Intelligence from 1973-1978 and was involved with a declassification team. Koi says that in 1974 he/she read a file from 1965 that started out as a criminal investigation of five army employees. Koi did not want to specify the nature of the investigation, but it was found that three of the five had links to certain people allegedly involved in the JFK assassination at Dealey Plaza, Dallas on 22 November 1963. So the story goes, based on the 1965 investigation, the three people were in Dallas on five occasions in the ten days leading up to the assassination, and each time were filming Dealey Plaza (this info supposedly came from another army informant), the grassy knoll, and the book depositary where Oswald supposedly was etc. what became of the films is unknown, but Koi claims suspicions were raised that they were made to give the real assassins a good layout of Dealey Plaza etc. Koi says nothing conclusive was ever proved, but all five men retired within 12 months from the army on various grounds. Koi says the file he/she read was shredded. That's it.

This was a new twist. Was Mrs Ingersoll something to do with the elusive Agent Koi? Maybe her husband - a US Government Foreign Office Attache (often, according to my Cold War spy thrillers, a euphemism for high ranking CIA operative) - WAS the elusive Agent Koi. Maybe she was Agent Koi herself? Unless this is all a coincidence, it seems certain that Agent Koi was involved far earlier than the Conspiracy Theorists now believe.

So there you have it. That is the entire story as far as I know it, and as far as Nick Redfern knows it. If Mrs Ingersoll is still alive (which is doubtful as she was considerably older than my late mother), I have no idea how to contact her. So the matter has to rest.

However, if any readers are ever in Hong Kong, go along to the LRC in Central District and see if the koi carp tanks are still there for me...

CHAPTER TEN
KOI ON MARS?

Mars is the fourth planet from the Sun in our solar system and is named after Mars the Roman god of war. Mars is also known as the "Red Planet" due to its reddish night time appearance when seen from Earth. The prefix *areo-*, from the Greek god of war, Ares, refers to Mars in the same way *geo-* refers to Earth. It is known as 火星 to the Chinese, meaning star of fire, and Mangala or Angaraka in Sanskrit In Indian languages like Hindi, telugu Tuesday is called *Mangalvaar* named after Mangala, Mars, and Bahram in Persian related to the Persian mythology.

Wikipedia – *The Free Encyclopaedia*

Anyone who read the previous chapter will know about my friend Nick Redfern – the shaven headed UFO expert from the West Midlands who to everyone's surprise (including, I suspect, his own), met a beautiful Texan lady called Dana and now lives in Port Arthur near Houston. He looks upon my activities with a detached amusement, and when I first started writing this column he refused to believe that there *could* be anything mysterious about koi carp. *"What? You mean those things that look like giant goldfish? Don't be silly"* he said to me the last time we met in the flesh.

However, a few issues ago he helped me with an article I was writing about Koi Carp at RAF Rudloe Manor in Wiltshire, and last issue, with the story of *Agent Koi* and the JFK Assassination, he provided most of the information. Much against his better judgement he has become more and more involved in my researches into the mysterious side of koi carp. The following story is *entirely* down to him!

In early April 2002 he sent me a cryptic e-mail:

Oi, Jon --- I bet U didn`t know that NASA were sending Koi Carp into space....

I had absolutely no idea and told him so so. I had a sneaking suspicion that he was taking the mickey, and subtly suggested as much. A few days later he replied mildly indignantly:

Yo Jonny, Here is the koi story for you. It's an extract from a Nasa archive web-site that deals with the Space Shuttle Endeavor, Mission STS-47, that flew into space on 12 September 1992 from the John F. Kennedy Space Centre. Here is what was on board the flight (extracted from the web):

*Materials science investigations covered such fields as biotechnology, electronic materials, fluid dynamics and transport phenomena, glasses and ceramics, metals and alloys, and acceleration measurements. Life sciences included experiments on human health, cell separation and biology, developmental biology, animal and human physiology and behavior, space radiation, and biological rhythms. Test subjects included the crew, **Japanese koi fish (carp)**, cultured animal and plant cells, chicken embryos, fruit flies, fungi and plant seeds, and frogs and frog eggs.*

Now why the hell would they be sending koi carp into space?

I assumed that the last question was a rhetorical one, and so I resisted the temptation to come out with a silly answer, and applied my energies to trying to get to the bottom of the conundrum. The first thing to do, of course, was to e-mail NASA. For some reason they didn't deign to reply. Ironically I have found it increasingly difficult to get any response from US Authorities since I made an off-colour joke about President Clinton on a live radio show in Nevada in 1999, but I'm sure that this is merely a coincidence.

So I had to try less conventional avenues of enquiry.

I'm really not more than tangentially interested in the subject of UFOs. However, I wrote a couple of books on the subject a few years ago when I was strapped for cash, and during my brief involvement with the subject I made quite a few friends who are interested in such things. These friends range from the barking mad, to the depressingly sane and all points in between. However between them they have a wide range of experience and knowledge. So I telephoned various people whom, I thought, might know why the American Government were sending koi carp into space.

STRENGTH THR⊕VGH K⊕I

The answers I was given ranged from the cor blimey to the ridiculous.

- Robin, an earnest young man with wild staring eyes and an unruly shock of hair muttered something about CIA funded black projects, and cyborgs, and then slammed the telephone down.

- `Crazy Dave`, from Bridgewater, the author of one of the most preposterous pieces of tripe that I had ever read on the subject of the so-called flying triangles, claimed that they were part of a secret State Department project to swap large amounts of DNA material from a wide variety of earth creatures for equally diverse DNA from creatures inhabiting an alien planet.

- Simon from Darlington, said that recently declassified US Goverment papers suggested that there had been a programme going on for years to preserve DNA from every earth species in a giant orbiting gene bank which would operate something like Noah`s Ark in the event of a global catastrophe. After the drivel that the previous two Informants had spouted, I was inclined to give this thory a little more credence, until he admitted that he had actually got the scenario from an old episode of *Star Trek* and there was no evidence whatsoever for his theory except that it sounded good.

Frustrated, I even asked my housemate Richard (an insane zoologist) if he had any ideas, and he spouted a long and complicated story about the US Government trying to breed a race of monstrous fish people, until we both burst out laughing and went down to the pub.

The next morning I received a rather smug e-mail from Nick.

Well, Jonny I think I`ve managed to solve it. I don`t know how true this is but there`s a guy I know vaguely over here who claims that he knows why the koi and the other biological material is being taken into space. He says that it is all to do with the long term Mars Exploration project. The long term aim of the project will be a permanent base on the planet and in order to do this they will have to establish a viable ecosystem. Because the genome of koi carp is relatively well known they are amongst the first creatures being considered for what in the long term will be the terraforming of Mars. I think you owe me a beer.....

This made a certain amount of sense, I thought, and certainly was the only explanation that anyone had come up with which wasn't obviously arrant nonsense. In the absence of anything better this explanation would have to do.

Just then my then-girlfriend walked into the room. She had recently started to tape large chunks of my CD collection to play on her walkman. She smiled at me as she walked past the desk where I was sitting at my computer. I caught a brief snatch of the song she was listening to. It was from a 1971 album called *Hunky Dory.* It was David Bowie singing *"Life on Mars"*.

I burst out laughing and decided that if that wasn't an omen then nothing was.

Chapter Eleven
Abducted!

David Bowie (born **David Robert Jones** on January 8, 1947) is an English singer, songwriter, multi-instrumentalist, producer, arranger and mixer, whose work spans more than four decades. A knowing, indulgent and occasionally camp figure, he is universally recognised as one of the more accomplished and inspired artists in popular music. Throughout the 1970s he took cues from art, philosophy and literature, and appeared to elevate popular music to a more sophisticated level while cleverly not overplaying the gravitas card. He is also a film and stage actor, music video director and visual artist.

Wikipedia – *The Free Encyclopaedia*

It is ironic that the last chapter ended with a reference to David Bowie, because "The Thin White Duke", is himself, indirectly responsible for this chapter's outing into the weirder side of the world of koi carp. For I have been a fan of David Bowie since the halcyon summer of 1973 when my mother made me wash off the glitter makeup, and wouldn't let me have *that* haircut. Readers of a certain age will know perfectly well what I mean, whereas those too young to remember the heyday of glam rock, will just sit back in bemusement at the idea that their elders and betters too, once put on stupid clothes and ponced about.

I'm too old and too fat to put on makeup and mince around in platform boots even if that was still *de rigueur* for David Bowie fans, but I still buy his albums when they come out (the 2002 CD, *Heathen* is brilliant by the way), and occasionally go and see him live when he tours. When my mate Richard Dawe telephoned me in late May 2002 to tell me that he had managed to obtain tickets to the first night of Bowie's *Meltdown* Festival at the Royal Festival Hall, I was only too happy to stump up my fifteen quid and go along with him. No matter that Bowie himself wasn't actually appearing, and that it was actually a classical concert featuring Phillip Glass's symphonies based around two of Bowie's albums. It was a day out, and an excuse for Richard to leave his wife and kids behind for the day, and for me to leave behind the trials and tribulations of running the world's only mystery animal research group.

As I sit typing this, my girlfriend is peering over my shoulder. *"What's David Bowie got to do with fish?",* she asked. I can imagine that thousands of readers of this book are asking the very same question, so I will tell you what I told her. *"Hold your whisht – I'm getting to that bit".*

We got to the Festival Hall, reasonably easily and ensconced ourselves in the bar. I was cheerfully tucking into a pint when a cheery voice came out of nowhere behind me. It was Billy, a geezer I have known ever since we worked together on one of the less reputable UFO magazines years ago. It turned out that he was also a David Bowie fan of many years standing and, pint in hand, he sat down to join us.

We chatted about David Bowie for a while, but none of us are fourteen any more, and the days of talking about our favourite pop star for more than five minutes are long gone, and so the conversation drifted desultorily towards our respective jobs of work. I mentioned that I was writing a regular column for *Koi Carp* magazine and almost in unison they both said *"I've got a story about koi carp that you can use if you like"*. We all laughed at the synchronicity of both of them saying the same thing at the same time, and – with my journalistic cap firmly on my head – I asked for their stories.

Richard spoke first. *"Well, its this bloke I used to work with"* he started. *"I used to work in this metalworking factory and there was a geezer who used to keep koi carp. But then he moved into a new house which had a much bigger pond in the garden. He introduced his beloved fish to the pond and they all started to disappear. He had dozens of them, but then each night one or two would go and over a period of a month he lost most of his fish. At first he thought that someone was stealing them, so he kept watch......"*

We sat back in our seats, enthralled. Richard has always had the gift of telling a story, and we were agog to see what happened next.

STRENGTH THROUGH KOI

"Well, he sat out for a couple of nights, but although he stayed awake all night looking at the pond no-one came. In the morning though, two more fish were gone!"

Apparently this bloke had seen a couple of owls flitting around during his midnight vigils and he wondered whether they could have been responsible for the predations. We sat back in our chairs laughing at the idea that there were owls big enough to carry off full grown koi flitting about the suburban skies each night. Richard laughed as well, but then he looked a little grave and continued.....

"Its not really funny. The poor chap was completely distraught. These fish were his pride and joy and they were disappearing as fast as he could put them into his pond. He was convinced by this time that owls were the cause of his fish disappearing and so he pinched a load of metal mesh and stuff from work and erected this amazing security net on a pergola over the top of the pond..."

He waved his arms around expressively as he described how his former colleague had constructed something that looked as if it were guarding a top secret military installation. We laughed, but were touched by the guy's plight. Despite the security net, the fish were still disappearing and so he began to investigate the possibility that the fish were being taken by other predators. First he thought that mink might be responsible, then herons, then cats, rats, dogs, and even otters. Each time he thought of another possible predator, he added a new security measure because he was so worried about the loss of his fish that he was prepared to go to any lengths in order to protect them. He spent most of his spare time over the next few weeks making his pond impregnable, so by the time he had finished, it had so many floodlights, safety nets, and security doors that it looked something akin to a POW camp in a WW2 movie.

But still the fish continued to disappear.

Then came the day that he only had one left. This was a venerable old fish that he had kept for years. Richard described it as being *"a bloody great thing speckled in black and white"* He had owned this fish since it was quite a tiddler, apparently, and he was very fond of it. He had been regularly restocking his pond from the local garden centre but this one fish had always managed to evade whatever it was that had caught all the others.

Then one morning, it too had gone.

Richard's erstwhile colleague was distraught. This was it, he decided, and he decided to drain the pond. He set the pump running, and drove down to the local garden centre where he had bought all his ill fated fish to tell them that he was giving up the hobby and to try and sell them a job lot of books and equipment. When he got there he was astonished to find his favourite koi carp, priced at a reasonable £500 swimming around quite happily in the huge concrete ponds which held the garden centre's stock.

He stormed into the office and confronted the Manager. *"What the bloody hell's my fish doing here?"* he fumed.

"YOUR fish?" he answered. *"It can't be – I've only just bought it"*. He gestured at a boy of about eleven or twelve who was wandering around in the water garden section trying his best not to look as if he were having lecherous thoughts about the terracotta statues of naked wood nymphs that were on sale therein. He was carrying a plastic cool box of the sort which some people take on picnics during hot weather.

"I bought it from him. I buy lots of fish from him"...

Without waiting to hear any more, Richard's friend rushed out to the small boy, grabbed him by the collar and unceremoniously dragged him into the office.

"`ere" said the boy indignantly, but Richard's colleague was adamant. *"How did you steal my fish?"* he asked sternly.

"I didn't steal no fish" he muttered indignantly. *"They were swimming in the pond in the park. Its public property, so the fish must belong to me as much as they do to anyone. I just catch them and bring them in here."*

By this time both the men were beginning to feel a little less angry, and were impressed by the lad's obvious sincerity. *"You'd better show us where you mean"*.

So the unlikely trio went down to the local public park where, sure enough, there were several large koi carp swimming happily amongst the shopping trolleys and duckweed.

Billy and I were completely enthralled. *"So how had they got there?"* we both asked.

It turned out that the solution to the problem was quite simple. The person who had originally built the pond in Richard's friend's garden had included a drainage pipe which led, underground into a culvert that eventually led into the feeder pipe for the pond in the park. When Richard's friend bought the house and installed the koi he had absolutely no idea that the mesh across the entrance to the waste pipe had corroded, and that just as fast as he had been putting koi into his pond, they were swimming out again to a temporary freedom. I say "temporary", because, no sooner had they arrived amongst the urban detritus of the city park, than the young lad was catching them and selling them back to the Garden Centre. Richard's friend and the bloke from the Garden Centre did a few calculations, and worked out that he probably bought the same fish several times over.

The mystery was solved. The three folk involved, apparently reached some sort of agreement as to who owed whom what and how much. They also agreed that no-one was to blame, and Richard's pal went home relatively happy.

That is..........

Until, on his arrival home, he was met by two burly policemen investigating the theft of large amounts of building materials, and was immediately arrested.

Billy and I almost fell of our seats laughing. Billy drew a breath and said *"That was amazing.. but I've got a koi carp story that will even top that"*

However, just then a voice came over the tannoy and announced that the show was about to begin. We wandered into the auditorium and found our seats. The concert was amazing, and in the interval, we met up with Billy back in the bar and he told us his koi story.

However, you lot, are going to have to wait until next chapter for that one!

CHAPTER TWELVE
BILLY'S STORY

Philip Glass (born January 31, 1937) is an American composer. His music is frequently described as *minimalist*, though he prefers the term *theatre music*. He is considered one of the most influential composers of the late-20th century and is widely acknowledged as a composer who has brought art music to the public (apart from precursors such as Kurt Weill and Leonard Bernstein), in creating an accessibility not previously recognised by the broader market.

Wikipedia – *The Free Encyclopaedia*

There is something about classical music, especially the sort of minimalist repetitive hypnotic stuff served up by Phillip Glass that always makes me thirsty. Therefore as soon as the first half of the concert at London's Royal Festival Hall was over my friend Richard and I made a bee line for the bar. There we found Billy, pint in hand, waiting to greet us.

As regular readers of this column will be aware, in last month's exciting episode I told the tale of how Richard (a mate of mine from our mutual mis-spent youth) and I had gone up to London to see a performance of two symphonies based on the music of David Bowie. "But what has this to do with fish?" I hear you ask.

While we were waiting for the performance to begin we ran in to Billy, another friend of mine, and in a scenario which might seem a little strange to people unfamiliar either with me and my friends or with the

STRENGTH THROUGH KOI

strange and often internecine world of koi carp, started talking about
our favourite fish. Both Richard and Billy had stories to tell me about
the weirder edges of koi-keeping, and in last month's column I retold
Richard's story about his ex workmate and the saga of his vanishing
fish. However there was not enough room in last month's column for
both stories and as Billy's tale was equally weird, equally interesting,
and to my warped sensibilities, just as amusing I held it over until this
month. So, gentle reader, imagine that you are in the bar at the Royal
Festival Hall, as one of my dodgier media pals regales us all with the
tale of Quentin, and his vanishing koi carp, not to mention the little
grey man from Zeta Reticuli who may or may not have been instru-
mental in removing them from his garden pond.

Billy took a swig from his pint of beer. *"Jon, you remember Quentin?"*
he asked me with a smile. I nodded. I did indeed remember Quentin
from my days working with Billy on various UFO related publications.
Quentin was a neurotic little man who wrote bizarre nonsense for one
of the more dubious magazines which was then being published on the
subject of flying sorcery and things that go whizz in the night. He was
obsessed with the idea that everything portrayed in *The X Files* was
the literal truth and that the British Government, the American Government and probably everyone else up to and including HM White
Fish authority and the DVLC in Swansea were in league with aliens
from Outer Space. He was also outrageously camp, and made Graham
Norton seem like Arnold Schwartzenegger in the butchness department. He lived in suburban Surrey with a succession of "special
friends" (all ruggedly good looking young men who robbed him blind)
and a large pond full of koi carp.

Quentin was actually a garden designer by trade, and although his
own garden was a riot of bad taste, which deserved to have been fea-
tured in one of the camper movies by John Waters, he was apparently
pretty successful at his chosen career. I visited him once to interview
him for a magazine which shall remain nameless, and we sat by his
ornate Japanese styled koi pond, complete with day-glo pagodas and
tiny mannequins dressed as Liberace, sipping sweet sherry and watching his beautiful koi carp swimming lazily up and down the blue green
depths of his pond.

Billy continued. *"Well apparently, during the summer of 1997 his koi
carp started to disappear".* The summer of 1997 had been the apogee
of media interest in the subject of unidentified flying whatnots. It was
the 50th anniversary of the Roswell Incident, the alleged "alien au-
topsy" footage was being bandied around the TV networks and you
couldn't walk down the street without seeing someone dressed in an
alien T-Shirt, or wearing a flying saucer badge. At least at first even
Quentin was not paranoid enough to link his disappearing koi carp in

with his obsession with flying saucers, but when, after a week or so, hardly a night went by without another one of his valuable fish disappearing without a trace, he began to put two and two together, and made six hundred and sixty-six. What didn't help was that at the very same time that Quentin's fish had been disappearing, there was a spate of UFO sightings in the very same leafy Surrey suburb in which he lived.

Every morning when Quentin opened the local paper, he would find that another weird light had been seen in the suburban sky the night before, and then - each morning as he took his constitutional wander around his garden - he would see that another one of his prized fish was missing. Like the gentleman I wrote about in the last issue, he originally thought that a heron might be responsible, but unlike the other gentleman he did not go to the lengths of turning his garden into a high security prison camp in order to protect his koi. After all, as each day passed he became more and more convinced that his koi carp were being stolen by aliens.

You might have thought that this knowledge would have perturbed Quentin? Not at all. He was overjoyed. According to his own personal cosmology, whilst the evil earth governments were definitely in league with evil aliens who were intent on subjugating humanity and making slaves of us all, there was another set of completely different aliens who were at war with the nasty aliens and were fighting for the forces of truth and light and the Galactic Federation blah blah blah.

By this time in the narrative, Richard looked at me with tears of amazement in his eyes. *"You mean people actually believe all this nonsense????"* he gasped. *"Of course they do,"* I laughed, *"How do you think I paid for my divorce? I wrote stuff like this for years, and people like Quentin KEPT on buying it"...*

As Richard drank his pint in stunned amazement, Billy continued his story. Apparently as soon as Quentin had decided that his carp were being stolen from his garden by benign folk from a galaxy far away, he decided to telephone all his friends. If the aliens were doing him the honour of stealing his fish, the least he could do was lay on a reception committee for them. Within hours the situation was completely out of hand.

Quentin's friends were all as equally deluded as he was, and each of them had a wide circle of likely minded acquaintances. By sundown that night there were well over a hundred people crammed into Quentin's admittedly not very spacious back garden. They were waving banners and chanting. Some of them had taken off their clothes and were dancing more or less rhythmically to the sounds of spacey electronic music, and with each hour that passed more and more people arrived and by midnight, when the police finally came, the party had overflowed out of Quentin's garden an d had spread into the road outside.

Three people were arrested for breach of the peace, and Quentin was questioned for several hours. When he had finally finished "helping the Police with their Enquiries" he was led out of the police station when he was shocked to see his latest "special friend" (a pretty young man called Barry), together with another man being led into the same police station.

"Bawwy......what is it? Have the aliens come after all?" Quentin was in tears at the thought that the aliens had finally visited his garden in person without him being there to greet them. The truth was, however, far more sordid.

The Police, having finally dispersed the chanting band of eager Alien watchers from Quentin's garden, decided to return to the scene a few hours later just in case there was any trouble. What they found was Barry, along with a "special friend" of his own emptying the remaining fish from Quentin's pond into polythene sacks in the back of a white mini van. It turned out that the whole affair had been nothing more than a particularly sordid scam on Barry's behalf. Even the UFOs had been fakes – nothing more than firelighters hoist aloft by toy balloons full of helium.

Despite laughing, I felt quite sorry for poor Quentin. *"What happened to him? He must have been gutted?"* I asked.

"Nothing of the sort" chortled Billy into his pint. The last time I saw him he had chucked in his job as a garden designer and was on a lecture tour of the United States with one of the policemen, and they were claiming that Barry was nothing more than a CIA mole sent in to stop the aliens landing in Quentin's back garden that night!

We nearly fell off our bar stools laughing at this final revelation, and no doubt the conversation would have gone on further if just then the bell hadn't rung to warn us of the imminent start of the second half of the evening's performance.

CHAPTER THIRTEEN
THE CURSE OF THE OWLMAN

Owlman, sometimes referred to as the **Cornish Owlman** or **The Owlman of Mawnan**, was a cryptozoological creature that was sighted in the late 70s in the village of Mawnan, in Cornwall.

Wikipedia – *The Free Encyclopaedia*

In the early summer of 1996, one of the strangest headlines ever to hit British newspapers was published. It read "Monster ate my fish", and told the story of a retired gentleman in the village of Mawnan Smith near Falmouth in Cornwall. For some weeks his koi carp had been disappearing and it had been suggested that the culprit may have been the Owlman of Mawnan - a semi legendary monster said to live in the woods around the village. Weight had been lent to the theory when, early one morning one of his neighbours had seen a gaunt, grey, feathered object flapping through the trees at the bottom of his garden.

Now, I was particularly interested in this story because, as some of you may know, back in 1996 I wrote a book called *"The Owlman and Others"* which covered the history of the Owlman phenomenon in tortuous detail. . I was particularly proud of the fact that I had received an award for "Best Paranormal Book of the Year" from the *Anomalist Magazine*, and in the wake of this and other accolades, I was particularly interested to follow up as many twists and turns of the story as I could.

The Owlman saga had begun on the Easter Weekend of 1976 when two small girls on holiday in Cornwall with their parents had been frightened by what one of them described as "a nasty grey bird man" that they had seen flying in the woods surrounding Mawnan Old Church. Over the next few years there were a number of other sightings - usually involving adolescent girls. Sally Chapman and Barbary Perry (both aged 14) saw it in July 1978, some unnamed French girls the same year, and by the time that a boyfriend and girlfriend (aged 12) encountered the fearsome phantom in 1989 there had been nearly twenty different eyewitnesses. The sightings slowed down in the 1990s but there were incidents in 1993, 1995, and 1997, and it seemed quite probable that here was another one.

I drove down to Cornwall that evening. Over the years I had visited the area many times and I was as familiar with the highways and by-ways of the little village on the Helford River as I am with my own suburb of Exeter. I know where each and every Owlman related incident had taken place, and it was pretty easy for me to find out where the alleged Owlman/Koi interaction had taken place.

I parked up in the car park at the old Church, and together with my old dog Toby (who sadly died, aged 15 in 2000), I quietly made my way across two fields to an old stile which was a convenient vantage point from which I could see both the garden pond from which the koi had allegedly been taken, and also the old church where most of the sightings had taken place.

It was a long, cold night. At about four in the morning, just before dawn I sat back, lit a cigarette, took a deep drag, and turned round to my dog. *"I'm getting too old to do this Toby"*, I said, and Toby scratched himself and yawned. There must be better ways to spend one's life, I thought. I was nearly forty years old, and here I was spending the night trespassing on the edges of someone's garden waiting for a mythical monster to attack some koi carp. I must be bloody insane!

Then, as the first fingers of pink began to illuminate the slate grey sky, I could hear the sound of beating wings in the sky above me. For the first time in the night, I was not just uncomfortable, cold and tired. I was scared. As the sky became lighter the sound of the beating wings became louder and suddenly I could see a great, grey, winged object alight next to the pond. Then it was joined by another one. Finally I knew the truth behind the mysterious disappearances of fish. There was indeed a mysterious pair of predators in the woods sur-

Fishy goings on in the garden pond? Blame the Owlman

By CHRISTOPHER EVANS

TO Roy Standring, the explanation for the regular disappearance of the goldfish from his garden pond was obvious.

Herons, he decided, must be to blame for the thefts. But locals in the Cornish hamlet had a more bizarre theory.

The fish, some claimed, were being preyed on by the Owlman of Mawnan — a 5ft tall half-owl half-man, a winged beast with red eyes and black talons.

According to Jonathan Downes, who studies such phenomena, the Owlman has appeared regularly to adolescent women in Mawnan churchyard.

Seventeen girls aged eight to 18 have reported sightings since 1976. The only boy to have seen the terrifying apparition was a 13-year-old — but he was with one of the girls at the time.

The Owlman never speaks or hoots. He hovers, does hiss sometimes and occasionally crackles 'like static electricity', says 38-year-old Mr Downes, who has recently published a book on the beast.

The first reports of an Owlman came when a family called Melling from the North of England were on holiday at Mawnan, which is four miles south of Falmouth.

The family's two daughters were playing in the graveyard of the 13th century church on Easter Saturday, 1976.

Suddenly, they fled screaming into the car park where their parents were unpacking a picnic lunch.

They told hysterical tales of a man covered in feathers flitting about.

The Mellings, so the story goes, reported their encounter to a local 'wizard' called Doc Shiels.

Shiels was already investigating — or, according to some, fabricating — reports of a sea serpent called Morgawr.

Other sightings of the Owlman followed, including one that July.

The most recent of which Mr Downes is aware was by an American student.

She reported: 'I experienced what I can only describe as a vision of hell.

'I was walking along a narrow track in the trees. I was

Shiels: Serpent hunter

halted in my tracks when about 30 yards ahead I saw a monstrous man-bird thing.

'It was the size of a man with a ghastly face, wide mouth, glowing eyes and pointed ears.

'I just screamed and turned and ran for my life.' Sightings

and tales of the owlman precede Mr Downes's interest in the case. He has interviewed the only male witness, who is now 22. Mr Downes says: 'He's terrified even now.'

While Mr Downes remains adamant that the Owlman exists, others vary from the sceptical to the incredulous.

As the Tourist Officer for Cornwall, Roy Standring might be expected to back a myth which would not only explain the disappearance of his goldfish but might also encourage visitors to the area.

However, he rejects the existence of the Owlman.

'We've got more than enough powerful legends in Cornwall from King Arthur to the standing stones,' he insisted

yesterday. 'We don't need any spurious ones.'

Part of landscape gardener Rod Good's job involves working up at the churchyard.

'I haven't seen anything supernatural,' said the 52-year-old.

'But there certainly is one spot just below the churchyard where the atmosphere is very strange.'

Sergeant Alex Johnstone of Devon and Cornwall Police sighed and said: 'The Owlman is a new one on me. I look forward to seeing the proof.

'I have heard of the Hairy Hand of Dartmoor, though.

'Funnily enough, that's an excuse frequently offered by people returning from licensed premises.'

rounding this mysterious and slightly sinister village. It was a pair of herons.

My work done, I went back to my car which was parked in the car park by the church. I drank a cup of coffee from my thermos and watched the rays of the new rising sun play around the tower of the old church. After a brief sleep the dog and I drove back to Exeter. On the way back we stopped at a roadside cafe for breakfast. Much to my mild embarrassment the girl behind the counter had read my book on the owlman and recognized me.

We got talking and I told her about my adventures of the night before. I told her that just because the fish had been taken by a pair of herons didn't mean that there was no truth behind the phenomenon as a whole. She agreed, but asked me whether as a man approaching middle age, I was ever sorry that I had dedicated my life to the pursuit of monsters rather than to more conventionally remunerative pursuits. Did I have any regrets?

"Regrets? I've had a few", I said. *"But then again, too few to mention"*...

We laughed, I paid for my breakfast, and ushering Toby into my car began the long drive back to Exeter.

CHAPTER FOURTEEN
THEY SAVED HITLER'S KOI

Honorary Aryan (German: **Ehrenarier**) is a term from Nazi Germany; it was a status granted by the Bureau of Race Research to people who were not considered to be biologically part of the Aryan race as conceived by the Nazis, but were granted an "honorary" status of being part of that race, for example because their services were deemed valuable to the German economy.[

Wikipedia – *The Free Encyclopaedia*

One of my favourite songwriters is a chap called Roy Harper. Sadly, he has had very little commercial success, and I think it is unlikely that anyone under the age of 35 (and quite a few readers over that age), will have actually heard of him. However, in a career which has lasted since 1964 he has recorded numerous albums of his idiosyncratic songs. One of my favourites is called *Loony on the bus*, in which he bemoans the fact that whenever he goes anywhere, and whatever he is doing, he has a tendency to become accosted by people ranging from the mildly eccentric to the certifiably insane who want to tell him their life story. I have always understood that particular song, because the same thing seems to happen to me with monotonous regularity.

In 2002 - as many readers may well be aware - I lead an expedition to Martin-Mere nature reserve in Lancashire. We were in search of a giant fish which had been reportedly attacking waterfowl overwintering at the reserve. We found the fish, identified it, and then came home again. However, we were amazed at the enormous amount of interest that this - seemingly quite innocuous - story seemed to me Ghana within the pages of the British press. As a result of this, only a few days after we had come back to our base in Exeter, my colleague and friend Richard Freeman and I found ourselves back in Lancashire to make a live broadcast from the side of the lake on breakfast television.

This necessitated Richard and me travelling up there the day before. We spent a the night at a hotel in Southport and as is our wont we spent most of the evening prior to the broadcast sitting cheerfully in the bar. We were reading an issue of *koi carp* magazine and drinking lager when an extraordinary pair of people approached us.

"Ere, you're the two lads who were chasing that bloody great fish?" said a small, wizened old man with an almost impenetrable Lancashire accent. He glared at us accusingly, as his companion - a young man with vicious eyes and a skinhead haircut stood just behind him, cleaning his fingernails with a fork that he had taken from the hostess trolley by the door. We gulped our beer and admitted that yes, indeed we were the people who had gone on a successful search for the monster of the Mere. *"Well you found it, what's you doing back here again?"* he asked in a slightly menacing manner. We explained about our imminent appointment with GMTV, and the atmosphere thawed somewhat.

"You mind if we join you?" the younger one asked, but the way that he asked it was phrased so that it wasn't really a question. Neither Richard nor I actually wanted company - we were tired, and all we want to was to drink, talk nonsense, and then retire to our respective hotel rooms. However it appeared that we were not going to be able to get rid of this unpleasant pair without an overt act of hostility, so we gestured to them are to join us.

The younger of the two picked up my copy of *Koi Carp* magazine. *"You interested in those big buggers?"* he asked, and before I could answer him he continued " I gotta story for you".

He though recounted a story, which is quite possibly the strangest, and most bizarre tale, which I have ever recounted in this column - and as regular readers will know that is saying something! I am repeating the story just as we were told it with no guarantees as to its veracity. All I would do is quote the old Latin - *vaverat lector* - let the reader beware!

The old man, whom - it must be said - looked even older once we could see him up close, claimed that before the second world war, as a young man, he had been a member of Sir Oswald Mosley's British Union of Fascists. When the organisation was declared illegal in 1940, alongside many other "blackshirts" he had been sent to the civilian internment camp on the Isle of Man. His brother, however (the younger man's grandfather), had - despite holding similar political views - to been an NCO in the British Army and had fought his way through the European campaign, finally ending up with the first British Regiment to enter Berlin in 1945.

"What would you say to me if I told your that I knew where the Fuhrer's pet fish were?" he grunted at me in a combative, and slightly menacing manner. My first reaction would have been to tell him to go away and stop bothering us with such arrant nonsense, but his nephew - with an ACAB tattoo on his forehead proclaiming to those in the know that all members of the constabulary have parents who were not united in the Holy Bonds of Wedlock - was threatening enough for us to decide that discretion was the better part of valour. Richard and I could probably have taken him, but brawling in hotel bars is not the way to best impress either the lasses or the powers that be at GMTV, so we shut up and letting go on with his story.

Apparently, so our unpleasant informant told us, during the late 1930s Adolf Hitler had granted "honorary Aryan" status to most of all the Japanese high command, including the God Emperor himself - Hirohito. As a riposte to this signal honour from their Axis allies, the Japanese royal family sent a number of gifts to the German leader. These included koi carp from one of the most ancient temples in the land of the rising sun. It is well known that Hitler was an animal lover. He had a dog called `Goldi`, and in many ways was a sensitive man. Apparently, he was so touched by the gift of the Royal fish that he had a special pond made in the Führer Bunker. Although, when he realised that the end of the Third Reich was nigh, he committed suicide - after first having made similar provision for his wife and dog, his fish survived, and were somehow smuggled back to England by the unpleasant old man's brother.

It so happens, that I know a reasonable amount about the last days the Third Reich, and I have to say that I have never heard anything about pet fish in the Reichskanzel. However I knew about the sad fate of Goldie, and about Hitler's affinity towards and sympathy for non-human life forms, so despite the fact that it seemed horribly unlikely - there was a certain ring of truth to it.

I asked what had happened to Hitler's fish. The younger of the two men glared at me. *"I've got 'em in my garden pond, haven't I?"* he said with a vicious scowl. Although, I didn't believe the story for a moment, I was interested enough to ask if it was possible for us to come and see them. After all, if the story is true, despite the historical importance of these fish they would be well over 70 years old, and would be an impressive sight.

However, they made it perfectly obvious that they were not going to accede to our request. Both Richard and I had long hair, and were obviously degenerates of the worst kind. These last survivors of the Third Reich had existed since 1945 in suburban Southport, and if their guardians had anything to do with it they would stay, in seclusion, for many more years to come. The unwarranted intrusion of people like us could only attract the wrath of left-wing activists who might harm the fish, or more realistically the military authorities who would want to impound them because of their undoubted historical and military interest. No, they were not prepared to tell us any more than they already had.

The bell for last orders rang, and we made our excuses and left. Was this extraordinary tale true? Could there be a valuable historical relic swimming peacefully in a pool in suburban Lancashire? Or were these two unpleasant characters just the latest manifestations of what Roy Harper meant when he sang *"Why do I always find myself next to the loony on the bus?"*

I doubt whether we will ever know the answer to either question.

CHAPTER FIFTEEN:
BIGFOOT AND THE POND FISH

Bigfoot, also known as **Sasquatch**, is the name of a phenomenon which
has polarized people around the world, being either the product of vivid
imagination or a creature that has somehow avoided close observation or
capture by man.

Wikipedia – *The Free Encyclopaedia*

In these pages, I have written many a story of koi carp which came
to an untimely end because of their interaction with a strange creature, a monster, or - allegedly at least - with a being from another
planet. As has been seen, on most of these occasions, the truth has
turned out to be far more prosaic, although quite often rather more
amusing. I am sure, that those few who used to read the little bit at
the end of last month's column where I always gave a teaser about
what would happen next month, (*Bigfoot and The Pond fish* in this
case) would have thought that they were in for much the same. As
soon as I mentioned Bigfoot and koi carp in the same sentence, I am
convinced that 90% of you reading this will have thought that they
could define the contents of this month's column in advance. You will
have thought that it was story of some backwoods fish keeper who
found that his koi were disappearing on a nightly basis, so he kept
watch only to find that it was Bigfoot eating his pond pets.

Wrong! In fact you couldn't be wronger.

STRENGTH THROUGH KOI

As many of you will know, I am the director of the Centre for Fortean Zoology - the world's only full time and professional scientific organisation dedicated to the study of unknown species of animal. One of the perks of my job, is that I get to travel all over the world both in search of strange creatures, and to lecture at conferences. During the summer of 1999 I was one of the speakers at the International UFO Congress, at Mesquite, Nevada. I am not the slightest bit interested in UFOs, but I wanted a free holiday, and was quite happy to give a lecture about strange animals found in the places where people had seen lights in the sky, in order to sing for my supper. I gave my lecture, and it went down reasonably well despite the fact that most of the audience were of the new-age type who tend to treat the study of UFOs as a religion, and have no sense of humour whatsoever. I have to admit that I spent most of my time in Nevada either sitting in the bar, or wandering around the campus looking at the local wildlife.

One night when I was in the bar, one of the locals came up to me.

"You one of them flying saucer people?" he said

"Errrm not exactly", I replied, and explained that I was a zoologist who had come all away from England to speak at the conference.

Over a few drinks we got talking, and my new friend asked me if I was interested in the subject of Bigfoot. I admitted that I was, and that the investigation into the fabled 8ft tall hairy manbeast of the Pacific north-west had interested me for some time. My new friend was quite drunk by this time, and he picked up his drink, leaned forward, and leered at me conspiratorially.

"You know that they ain't normal animals at all..." he whispered, and my heart sank. So, this is why he had sought me out as one of the " flying saucer people", he was just another nutter who was going to tell me that Bigfoot came from The Planet Zog, and that he had personal knowledge of this after having been abducted. But I was wrong.

He blushed.

"I seen one once", he told me - almost embarrassed to have let a total stranger in on one of the deepest secrets of his life. I had to coax the story out of him but he told me how his brother lived outside one of the small villages about 40 miles from Seattle and how he had - many years before - spent a week visiting him. It turned out that his brother was somewhat of an eccentric who lived in a tar paper shack, with a couple of large hunting dogs for company. The shack had beautifully landscaped gardens featuring two lovely koi ponds, but otherwise was extremely rudimentary and didn't even have the benefit of electricity

or modern plumbing facilities. One night, my friend, was taken short and had to answer a call of nature in the tiny, malodorous, shed at the bottom of the garden. He was making his way back up to the main house when he saw what he thought was his brother sitting on a rock by the side of the larger of the two koi ponds. He ambled over to say hello when the figure stood up, and he could see that it was not his brother - it was a shambling figure between 7 and 8 ft tall covered in hair and with bright red eyes.

It was hard to know which of the two figures, and each ran in opposite directions. My new friend stumbled back to his brother's shack, to find his brother sitting calmly in a rocking-chair by the fire. He told him of his encounter, but his brother was not all surprised. It turned out that the Bigfoot was a regular visitor to the koi pool. My friend asked whether any of his brother's prized fish had gone missing. His brother nodded his head and said that quite the opposite took place. On several occasions, he said, he had surreptitiously watched as the huge, hairy biped sat on the rock, leant forward and gently scooped the water into his enormous cupped hands.

"Its the dangdest thing", he told my friend, *"one of my biggest and most beautiful fish jumped into his cupped hands and the two animals just sat there looking at each other before he let the fish back into the water"*.

Apparently this has happened on several occasions, and although my friend never saw it for himself, he saw the giant 8 ft shadow shambling around in the darker recesses of the garden twice more before he left to return home.

"So that's why I say he isn't an ordinary animal", he muttered, *"I don't what he is but an ordinary animal would have eaten the fish...."*

We finished our drinks in silence, and I went to pay a call of nature myself. When I returned he was gone. It was only then that I realised that if the story *was* true then, possibly the most extraordinary part was fact that the fish had seemed to have been quite happy to initiate contact with the man-beast.

As with many of the other stories in this column, I pass it on to you - the reader - as it was told to me. I take no responsibility to whether this or any of the other stories are true, but there are so many of them, and I got so many e-mails from readers giving me even more stories, that it does make one start to believe that koi carp are a very peculiar fish indeed.

STRENGTH THROUGH KOI

CHAPTER SIXTEEN
THE KILLER IN THE GARDEN

Walsall is the administrative headquarters of the Walsall Metropolitan Borough. In the 2001 census, the town had a population of 170,994 with the surrounding borough having a population of 252,800. Neighbouring towns in the borough include Willenhall, Bloxwich and Aldridge.

Wikipedia – The Free Encyclopaedia

In the year or so that I wrote this column, I received a number of emails giving me interesting little snippets. In 2003 I received a number of accounts of sightings of strange creatures which have – allegedly at least – been attacking koi carp in garden ponds. The most recent came from a story in a west Midlands newspaper which told the sad tale of Janet and John Newell of Walsall who complained that their prized collection of fish were being systematically snaffled up by a hungry and mysterious creature which makes raids from a nearby canal bank. Over a number of occasions in mid July this year something has been raiding their garden and dozens of comets, goldfish and koi carp have been eaten by the animal which Janet and John believe may be an otter. One 24-inch koi carp which the Newells had bought as a baby but was now worth £300 alone was butchered and eaten. The couple, of Sutton Road, Walsall, watched in horror as the creature dived into the pond, seized the fish and made off with it. According to the original account the fish then became caught in a hole in the garden fence and the animal kept coming back to take the occasional nibble.

The bank leading from John Newell's
back garden down to the canal

John Newell

John Newell's pond

The canal

John shows Richard Freeman where the
attacks took place

"It's an otter!"

"Up until then we had not seen the creature although we knew some-thing was taking the fish and eating them," said 56-year-old Mrs New-ell. "We had assumed it was a feral cat but it was brown and cream in colour with very short legs and from what I have seen on television it looked like an otter. But we have been told that otters do not breed in or inhabit urban areas like this so what it actually is remains a mys-tery."

Their house backs on to a stretch of the Birmingham Canal and it is thought the mystery creature may have made its way down towards their home from the Park Lime Pits at Rushall. Officials from both the town's Countryside Rangers group and from British Waterways believe a mink may to be blame for the slaughter but Mrs. Newell was so adamant in maintaining that the animal was an otter, that we felt that we had to investigate for ourselves. *"They have not seen the creature and are going on educated guesswork,"* she said. They have now filmed the creature and are awaiting confirmation that, although they have been unlucky enough to lose a whole collection of their prized fishes, that they are lucky enough to have seen one of the few speci-mens of this rare and beautiful mammal that is beginning to recolonise the country.

We traclked down the Newells who by this time were heartily sick of the whole affair. They had been vilified and treated like idiots by the press and pretty well everyone else involved. With a defensive and slightly wary air Mr. Newell showed us the long, steep bank behind his house which leads down to the canal. The last time I had visited this stretch of the canal (nearly 20 years ago), it was a complete mess and somewhat reminiscent of an open sewer. Now it is a haven for water birds and fish and is carpeted by great, yellow, water lilies.

He showed us the gap in his fencing where the body of his big koi had been wedged and where the mystery beast came back day after day to feed. He showed us the well kept koi pond in the corner of his pretty little garden – an oasis for wildlife in the middle of a grey and slightly dull city, and finally he showed us the video he had taken. It showed...

... an otter.

It was unmistakeable. For the first time in well over a century otters had recolonised that part of Staffordshire. We watched the five minute film over again. We were overawed to see something so beautiful and graceful in the middle of the city. We took our photographs, shook Mr Newell's hand and left.

The mystery was solved.

That afternoon we drove twelve miles north to Cannock where another mystery awaited us. It also involved koi carp but you will have to wait for next time to hear about that one!

CHAPTER SEVENTEEN:
A FISHY JOHNNY APPLESEED

Cannock Chase is a mixed area of countryside in the county of Staffordshire, England. The area has been designated as the **Cannock Chase Area of Outstanding Natural Beauty**. The Chase gives its name to the Cannock Chase local government district.

Wikipedia – *The Free Encyclopaedia*

One of the best known legends of the American West is that of Johnny Appleseed. John Chapman, was born on September 26, 1774 near Leominster, Massachusetts. By the time he was 25 years old, he had become a nursery man and had planted apple trees in the western portions of New York and Pennsylvania. Some of the orchards in those areas were said to have originated with his apple trees. When the rich and fertile lands lying south of the Great Lakes and west of the Ohio river were opened for settlement in the early 1800's, John Chapman was among the very first to explore the new territory. This was the Northwest Territory from which the states of Ohio, Michigan, Indiana, and Illinois were later formed. For nearly half a century Johnny Appleseed roamed his territory. When settlers arrived, they found John Chapman's young apple trees ready for sale.

In the years that followed, he became known as the Apple Tree Man, or Johnny Appleseed. His manner of operation was simple. He went into the wilderness with a bag of apple seeds on his back until he found a likely spot for planting. There he would clear the land by chopping out weeds and brush by hand. Then he planted his apple seeds in neat rows and built a brush fence around the area to keep out straying animals. His nurseries varied in size. Some were only an acre or so, others covered many acres. He did all of the work himself, living alone for weeks at a time with only the Indians and wild animals for companionship. There is only one problem with this lovely story - it almost certainly never happened. However it is a nice myth and one which probably has a kernel of truth in it somewhere.

However, in 2003 I discovered that there seems to be a real-life analogue of Johnny Appleseed at work in the West Midlands. However, this man (or woman) isn't distributing apple seeds. He or she seems to be introducing koi carp to a ridiculously large number of bodies of water. In late July I led a trip to Cannock in Staffordshire where there had been sightings of a crocodile-like creature in a large pond. Now, I am not for a moment suggesting that crocodiles are an living and breeding in the waterways of the West Midlands. Far from it. However, crocodilians of several species are relatively easy to obtain on the black market and it seems quite probable that they could live for short times in British waters - at least during the summer months. We spent several days in the vicinity and as well as eye witness accounts of the crocodile we also received a number of reports from local anglers who had caught enormous koi carp in the pond.

Deciding that it made sense to consult an expert, we visited C.D Aquatics on the outskirts of town. There we spoke to Debbie Burns, one of the partners. They had a nice selection of koi as can for sale and obviously knew a lot about the subject. Not entirely to our surprise, she, too, had heard about the strange appearance of these magnificent fish (and anomalous alligators), in the pond at Roman View. She told us that we were not the first people to question her about the subject and intimated that even the police were interested.

We concluded our business at the pond in Cannock the next day and moved operations to the middle of Cannock Chase itself. The chase is an ancient stretch of woodland deep in the heart of the West Midlands. We were there with an electronic magnetometer doing our best to measure fluctuations in the EMF fields across the region. After a hard and long day wandering about in the rain we converged upon the Cannock Chase visitors' centre for a cup of tea. While we were there, several of our party got into a conversation with the local wildlife wardens about some of the unusual creatures that had been reported across the chase. There were accounts of muntjac deer, mystery panthers, exotic reptiles - and... you've guessed it koi carp. Apparently, or so they told us, koi carp had turned up in a number of ponds and streams across the Forest. And, just like back at the pond in Cannock, nobody knew who was putting them there.

Since our return to Exeter we have heard a number of other accounts of anomalous koi carp appearing in ponds across the West Midlands. Although we have no evidence to support this idea, it is tempting to theorise that there is a modern-day John Appleseed who, entranced with the beauty of koi carp, has decided to share his love for these gracious fish with the general public by introducing them to as many waterways as he can manage. Although as a zoologist I should not approve of anybody who is flouting the Wildlife and Countryside Act of 1980 and introducing alien species into the British environment, I too find koi carp ridiculously attractive, and hope that our modern-day Johnny Appleseed will carry on his good work for many years to come.

EPILOGUE

Email received: 08 September 2003 14:55

Hi Jon,

I thought I'd better send you an email regarding kurious koi.

You've probably noticed that we haven't published your articles for a couple of issues of the magazine. This is for two reasons. Firstly at this time of year the mag gets thinner, and we are very short of space - unfortunately it is the more light hearted types of article that suffer in the culling that goes on. The other problem is that the recent articles have only been very tenuously linked to koi, and really, although they make a diverting read generally, they don't really have much bearing on koi keeping.

Mark has asked that we put the kurious koi chronicles on hold indefinitely. This is not a reflection on your writing, it's simply that we are taking a slightly different direction with the mag - you know how it is in publishing, things are always changing! I think he wants to move away from the fictional/fantasy aspect, and focus more on the serious sides of the hobby.

I'm sorry that we can't use the two articles that you recently sent to us. If you want to discuss this, feel free to give me a call.

Thanks for the previous articles that you have provided for us - keep up the hunt for mysterious animals!

Kind regards

Louise

...................and the last two stories were completely true!

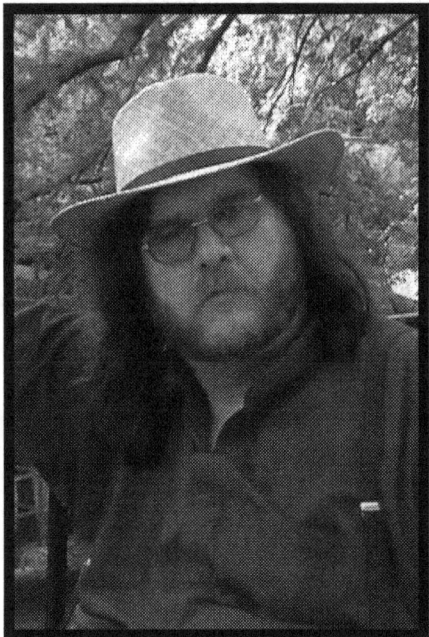

Jonathan Downes was born in Portsmouth in 1959, and spent much of his childhood in Hong Kong where, surrounded by age-old Chinese superstitions and a dazzlingly diverse range of exotic wildlife, he soon became infected with the twin passions for exotic zoology and the paranormal which were to define his adult life. He spent some years as a nurse for the mentally handicapped but began writing professionally in the late 1980s. He has now written over twenty books. He is also a musician and songwriter who has made a number of critically acclaimed but commercially unsuccessful albums.

In 1992 he founded The Centre for Fortean Zoology, with the aim of coordinating research into mystery animals, bizarre and aberrant animal behaviour and his own particular love of zooform phenomena (paranormal entities which only appear to be animals!)

He has searched for Lake Monsters at Loch Ness, pursued sea serpents and the grotesque Cornish owlman—which inspired his most famous book *The Owlman and Others* - chased big cats across westcountry moorland, and in 1998 and 2004 went to Latin America in search of the grotesque vampiric Chupacabra. He is a popular public speaker both in the UK and the United States, where he regularly appears at conventions talking about his many expeditions and his latest research projects.

He is also an activist for Mental Health issues, having suffered with Bipolar Disorder (Manic Depression) for many years. In 2005, after having lived in Exeter for 20 years, he moved to his old family home in Woolsery, North Devon, where he intends to establish a full-time Visitor's Centre and museum for the Centre for Fortean Zoology. Following his father's death in February 2006, he inherited the old family home and announced that construction of the museum and research facility later in the year.

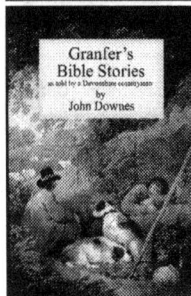